As for
Me and
My House

education is important

Rose Marie Whiteside

Copyright © 2011 by Rose Marie Whiteside

Rose Marie Whiteside
Visit my website at www.as-for-me-and-my-house.com

Printed in the United States of America
First Printing: March 2011

ISBN: 978-0615455839

To my family.

In memory of my deceased parents, Arthur and Maude Whiteside, providers of my genes; my living sisters, Naomi (Whiteside) Hughes, Selma (Whiteside) Van Ness and brother, Chester Whiteside;

Ashley Dunham, my son; Laurie Biederman, my son's significant other; Keyla Demetrie Dunham and Constance Spell Dunham, my granddaughters, and their mothers, Lois Mathis and Shawndalyn Feagins.

Arthur, like Joshua, always lived through the words "As for me and my house, we will," and in doing so passed it on to all of us.

Acknowledgments

I would like to express my gratitude to the following people who helped to make this book a reality:

My researcher, extraordinaire, J. Aype and my, unique/patient, editor Thomas Hauck, who have been with me from GPS to GPS.

The fearless students and parents from the Alternate Learning Program (ALP) located at the Claverack branch of the Hudson, New York – City School District – 2000.

The teachers with whom I worked in my capacity as the Coordinator of the ALP program including Janet Brust, Lance Wheeler, Ernie Reis and Fran Heaney. What a team!

It is because of all of you that this book even exists, for I drew the inspiration from each of you and my FAITH to write it.

Thank you one and all.

Contents

Part Three: What Shall We Do?

Introduction

Parenting is like a road trip. Before you begin, you must know where you're going. You have to have a destination or you'll never know if you arrived. Along the way, you need to look for familiar landmarks and road signs that indicate you're still on the right path. You also have to make certain you've meticulously followed the directions to your destination or you'll end up lost in a small town nowhere near your goal.

As For Me and My house: Education Is Important uses 38 GPS (Global Positioning System) locations. The content in each of these locations is free standing and does not necessarily connect with each other. Consider it a smorgasbord of thoughts and ideas on a variety of issues touching both public and private education today. Pick and choose what you want, need, or taste it all. Simply get in where you fit in.

Facts and studies are sprinkled throughout the content and come from Internet research. None is profound or earthshaking, but is included for those who may wish to research the area more thoroughly.

The locations are further broken up into three parts.

Part I – The House examines the effect of family values, race, religion and ethnicity on educational issues by looking at social standing, lifestyle, economics, expected outcomes, realities and roadblocks. Part II – Taking Action questions whether education should be a right or a privilege and examines alternative programs that might be more empowering for those who are not succeeding in the present system. Part III – What Shall We Do looks at a variety of issues briefly including racism, homeschooling, bullying, addictions, technology, use of the political system, sexuality, and others.

Although education is global in nature, what is happening

throughout the United States is the focus.

Some comments push the envelope to encourage a response to defend, agree or think about what is happening or not happening in education within our cities and states. The book's content is ready for a conversation that can occur within workshops, discussion groups, town hall meetings, or within living rooms around the country.

As a parent, evaluation of your own actions, beliefs and goals is always important. If you want to make certain you're going in the right direction, take time to reflect on the activities of your day, your week, or your month.

The end-point of your trip—your destination—is to have raised a well-educated child with moral values and a good work ethic. Everyone wants his or her child to succeed but often sees a prestigious job as an indicator of that success. In reality, a child brought up with virtue, belief in himself or herself, and the desire to do the right thing in life is really what every parent secretly hopes will be the end result. A child raised to have sound moral fiber, a good work ethic, self-responsibility, and caring parents can't help but to achieve his or her goal.

The child may not have a prestigious or high-paying job. However, you'll raise a responsible adult and no matter what he or she does, he or she will do their best at it. In our world there is no job that's inherently more important than another one. The past shows us that even a humble carpenter made a difference that changed history.

Along the way of the journey to your child's adulthood, you'll find many detours and confusing road signs. Sometimes, you'll have to stop and examine GPS directions carefully and make amendments. At other times, asking for directions can make the difference whether you find yourself lost or simply a little out of the way. No matter what, you're still in charge of the driving and the path you take.

The trip can seem endless at times, but at those times, you need to reflect on how far you've come. Take time from the trip occasionally to stop at one of life's roadside parks and enjoy the sweetness of the journey. You can linger a while because you have the knowledge that your family deserves to have the time together and enjoy the sweet scent of the flowers along the way. Just like any road trip, there are traffic jams, construction and bad drivers. Avoid getting angry but deal with each diversion as you come to it. If you find another parent is a "bad driver," don't become a parent with "life road rage." Simply stay on course and the problem will soon disappear.

Preface

It is common knowledge that in America today, public education is in trouble. For verification of the troubling downward trend we need only look at some basic statistics.

In 2009, the Program for International Student Assessment (PISA) surveyed fifteen-year-old students in 65 developed nations. PISA found that in literacy, U.S. fifteen-year-olds ranked seventh, scoring below Korea, Finland, Canada, New Zealand, Japan, and Australia.

In science, U.S. students ranked thirteenth, behind Finland, Japan, Korea, New Zealand, Canada, Estonia, Australia, the Netherlands, Germany, Switzerland, the United Kingdom, and Slovenia.

In mathematics, U.S. students ranked a dismal eighteenth among developed nations. We were lower than Korea, Finland, Switzerland, Japan, Canada, the Netherlands, New Zealand, Belgium, Australia, Germany, Estonia, Iceland, Denmark, Slovenia, Norway, France, and the Slovak Republic.

The causes of this poor performance are many, and in the years to come the consequences will be very real. In seeking solutions, this book's primary focus is on parents, for it is they who have ongoing responsibility for their children's education. They are the lynchpin for their children's education.

This responsibility is laid out throughout the pages and encourages parents to be engaged to ensure the best education for their children.

The inclusion of more parent involvement in the education process fills what can be the missing link in an educational system that is flawed and continues to remain so.

It is the intent of this book to change behavior of all players in the education process, and in particular that of the parents. Techniques to be used in this change are explored in this book and become part of the expected outcomes to be fulfilled.

Full inclusion of parents in the education process is a key plank in the federal No Child Left Behind law. Yet, throughout the country it appears that parents have little more than the handouts prepared by the federal government. These handouts speak of parent options and need for inclusion. However, the lack of full inclusion of parents in the education process continues to contribute to public school failure.

From one side of the country to the other, parents relate stories of being left out of their children's education process. Children's behavior problems are not mentioned until out of control. Bad grades suffer a similar fate.

SAT scores rendering less than the expected outcome serve notice that, for far too many, public schools are in disarray.

Public schools contain many landmines that are ready to go off when stepped upon. The poorly cared-for buildings, the unqualified teachers, the self-perpetuating unions, or the choice of curriculum and methodology can each trigger an explosion.

Therefore, it's time that the public education system responds to the need of every child who walks through its doors.

Let it really be true that No Child Is Left Behind.

To that end, *As For Me and My House* suggests that parents become empowered and take their rightful places alongside their children and the teachers. Each in his or her way is responsible for the end result. But it is the parent who has 24/7 decision-makings regarding his or her child.

Even though parents are not in a classroom, they are their children's first teachers. They model and the children follow their lead. Bragging to each other, parents know the first word that their children ever spoke, when they walked, and what strokes turn them on. This wealth of parent knowledge represents a gold mine.

That the public school system has a life of its own and shuts out the much-needed input of parents is unfortunate. But parents need not think that such input gives them an adversarial role. Instead, as part of the troika of the parents, children, and teacher, each has certain unique functions that only they can do within the process.

Instead of the school doing its thing, the student his or hers, and the parents standing on the outside looking in, advanced thinking would have these three represent a troika within the public school system with clearly defined roles that contribute to school excellence.

Right now, the school systems entertain the traditional PTA functions and in some areas have thrown in parent resource centers. Such centers are planned to assist parents with issues that they may have with the school and student problems. Critics see this as a pacifier to keep parents in check.

Unfortunately, there is not a true role for the parent who is the most important person in a child's life. Regrettably, they are the missing link in the chain.

If parents are more involved, early on, children are readied for the school experience and discipline problems can be resolved up front. This provides the teacher with more time to focus on curriculum and teaching.

The child represents the common denominator between the parent and the school. Doesn't it make more sense that the three would work together more closely?

Without the parent there is no child. Without support from parents, kids are left to deal with school issues on their own. Many parents only know of what goes on in the school setting if there are disciplinary problems or report card issues.

And, of course there is always Parent's Night. Enough said.

Part One:
The House

GPS 1: Joshua's House

Joshua 24:14-15 expressed specific role identification within the community and the family. The entire quote is thus:

> 14 Now fear the LORD and serve him with all faithfulness. Throw away the gods your forefathers worshiped beyond the River and in Egypt, and serve the LORD. 15 But if serving the LORD seems undesirable to you, then choose for yourselves this day whom you will serve, whether the gods your forefathers served beyond the River, or the gods of the Amorites, in whose land you are living. But as for me and my household, we will serve the LORD.

When Joshua spoke these words, God had kept his covenant with the Israelites. They had been delivered to Canaan and life was better for them.

What Joshua wants to know is how the Israelites will repay Yahweh for doing that. Will they remember Him, worship Him, and serve Him? Joshua reminds the people they have a choice of whom to worship but there must be no sitting on the fence. They worship either Joshua's God—Yahweh—or another God. There's no in-between.

Joshua gave them a choice and, in the manner of the times, made the decision for his household. Even though in that day and age there was the prodigal son, just as today, the parents had control over what was allowed in the house. Joshua gave each person the dominion over what occurred in the house and whom each family worshipped. He didn't order the others to make *his* choice, he simply told them to decide something and make it the choice for their families.

What Joshua said has meaning for us today. Our public schools are failing and each person is responsible for his or her part in that failure. You cannot legislate morality any more than you can mandate good behavior or the ability to learn, but taking an active part in the system and making certain that your family plays its role can make a difference. Just like Joshua, you cannot speak for the families of others but you can make your own family accountable for its actions.

GPS 2: Other Houses

Accountability isn't just relegated to the Judeo-Christian ethics or the Old Testament and Joshua. All religions, and even those people without religion, believe in a code of ethics, whether spoken or unspoken. While agnostics don't acknowledge either the existence or lack of existence of a supreme being, and atheists say there is no God, accountability to yourself for your actions and the ultimate price paid for the course you take in life is proof enough that personal responsibility is important. Even though the belief system of organized religion doesn't provide a guideline for agnostics and atheists, our innate understanding of right and wrong provides it.

The Jewish religion has the High Holiday, Yom Kipper, and Rosh Hashanah, which are all about personal responsibility and taking accountability for one's actions. The Ten Days of Repentance are a time when Jews acknowledge their sins and their shortfalls, and hold themselves accountable for the misdeeds of the year. This period of personal accountability also transfers throughout the year and daily life. It is the basic tenet that should be used for all parts of life, including schoolwork and behavior.

The religion of Islam views the parents in much the same role as Christian or Jewish families. The followers of Islam—Muslims—firmly believe in submission to the will of God. The Holy Koran (Quran) outlines how that is to be accomplished. While most people know that Islam follows the teachings of the Koran, few are aware that Islam recognizes other holy books, referred to as the scriptures. In addition to the Quran from Mohammed, these books include the Torah from Moses, the Psalms from David, and the Gospel from Jesus. Since these scriptures are included in the belief system of Islam, Joshua's

House is not a foreign belief to Muslims but very close to that of Christians and Jews.

Muslims learn early that each person is responsible for his or her own actions. While the Day of Judgment might be a long time away from the day of the classroom, the teachings of Islam emphasize that since God knows all action thought and deed, human beings should always be striving for their best behavior and will be held responsible.

Buddhism places personal responsibility and accountability on a high level, equal or higher than other religions. One of the beliefs of Buddhists is that ignorance brings suffering. Since the school system is one way to obliterate ignorance, Buddhist parents should, by the nature of their religion, hope their young charges learn as much as possible.

However, the key to the association of this religion to holding the student accountable for their actions is the belief that by taking responsibility for the actions and your own reality, you no longer become a powerless pawn blaming your victimization on the universe but now have control over your own suffering. This belief in personal responsibility transfers easily to grades and success in school. No longer does Johnny have the excuse that the teacher simply "gave" him a bad grade. He must look at his participation in the receipt of the grade. His parents share the same viewpoint that since it is their belief that your own actions are part of the ultimate outcome.

A firm belief in the Hindu religion is also in support of personal responsibility. The Vedic view is that if one does his or her own duties properly, it also fits and fulfills the rights of others. Since the Hindus have a belief in personal interdependence, there is no self-centered demand that any one person's rights are supreme to another. With this in mind it is easy to see how following the social structure, rules and regulations in the classroom would also follow the teachings of the religion.

A high value on knowledge and learning has always been prized among the followers of the Hindu religion. It was one method that served as a path to self-realization and therefore the highest end of life. India, in fact, was one of the few countries where they systematized knowledge in early times, making it easier to transfer to future generations in a detailed manner. As early as 800 B.C. India had a university that was similar to the modern-day universities. Education is considered noble and the highest goal. When you combine the belief in the importance of education and the sense of personal responsibility, it is easy to see why India, a land where Hinduism is most prevalent, often surpasses America in excellence in the schools.

While basing many of the ideals on the Biblical verse pertaining to Joshua's house and his belief that he was responsible for those in his house and their behavior, it is easy to say that this also translates to other belief systems, religious writings and upbringings. Every religious person, and even those whose religion is the absence of religion or atheism, understand that ultimately people are responsible for their lives because of the path they take. They don't need to worry about punishment in the afterlife (even though many do) to believe that everyone should be accountable for his or her actions. Even Wicca, one of the world's oldest religions, believes men and women are accountable for their lives and actions.

If both religious and secular parents would stand up and speak their belief that holding accountable all people involved in the educational system—teachers, students, administrators and parents—America would no longer be lagging behind. The problem is no one wants to speak out and it is far easier to blame another for the failings of the child rather than look at the situation and ask what you could have done as a parent to make your child more accountable. Until we see the problem as every person's, our system will continue to decline.

Today

The relevance of the Joshua quote and other religious beliefs still stands today. It doesn't matter what you believe in when it comes to your children—you must take a stand and live that belief. Each person will have a different view of education but without voicing his or her opinion and standing by his or her convictions, it leaves the schools in the hands of those vociferous people who may have dramatically opposing views on the subject.

Today there are school corporations that introduce condoms to first graders and suits against teachers because they attempt to maintain class control. You may find it appalling and shake your head—but do you stand up for what you believe? Do you take stock in Joshua's words and choose a side for your family to follow? The lack of good people taking a side is clearly where our school system began to decay, just as the lack of enforcing the belief in the home was the beginning of the decay of the family.

In today's society, it is becoming increasing more difficult to voice an opinion. If you disagree with President Obama or school busing, suddenly you're a racist. If you want to see stricter discipline in the schools, you have no empathy for the poor children that have no discipline at home or are simply acting out their home problems. People who set a mark in the sand or have strict moral convictions are viewed with disdain as inflexible. Because of this, the decay of our schools and way of life continues.

Like Joshua, I call to you to make a decision. What do you want from the educational system? What learning takes place in schools where the children have no restraint? It doesn't matter what your belief is—stand up and let your voice be heard. You have the responsibility of choosing for your house and if you don't, you've made the decision to follow the beliefs of others.

GPS 3: Family Structure

You have a choice in what you value, what you revere, and what you believe. You reveal that choice by the decisions you make, the items you purchase, and the way you spend your time. Just as Joshua called the Israelites to take a stand for one religion or another, you also must decide what your belief is and take a stand for your family values and choices.

What you choose for your family and children indicates your values. Why is the decision so important? Once you make a clear-cut choice for your belief, you then—and only then—establish the path to follow. Without making that decision, you wander aimlessly and eventually follow the easiest route established by others.

Can you thrust your views upon others? No, according to Joshua; you can only decide them for your house. However, in today's society, with lawsuits and injunctions many people do thrust their beliefs onto others. The ACLU not only sued the Santa Rosa School District because two atheist students said Christian teachers "witnessed" during class, but also demanded a Consent Order. The school agreed to the Consent Order and the Pensacola Federal District Court in Florida, entered it. This order prevented the teachers and school personnel from praying at any off-campus events even if the school didn't sponsor them. They sued two administrators for breeching this and praying and one teacher for having her husband pray in her stead.

After a legal battle, the teachers' rights to a private belief were reinstated. This, however, is just one example of people choosing how others should believe. Joshua did not presume to make that choice in Joshua 24:14-15 but simply called for each person to make his or her own decision on values and belief. Just as you have no right to impose your views on another, no one has a right to impose theirs on you.

Is it possible in today's world to set family values and stick to choices that fit in their design? The answer is, "Absolutely yes!" It is not easy, for there are spoilers out there as exampled above, but you must do it for the sake of your family. Without a belief system of some type, there is no destination and therefore there is no map.

On a television talk show, a single mother and her daughter of six or seven years old were at odds with one another. It seems the woman did not agree with her daughter's selection of mature and sexy-looking clothing. The daughter insisted on wearing them. If the mother had set values for the house, the clothing would never have been purchased. She had set no discipline for the child or boundaries; if she had, the clothing, had it been a gift, would have been returned. This mother did not decide the moral values of her home or take responsibility to make certain they were followed. The choice to allow the clothing in the home was hers and hers alone.

Every day parents shrug their shoulders and complain about the school not teaching their children discipline. In reality, it is their responsibility to teach discipline at home, even before the children entered school. If the child doesn't study, rather than wait for the schools to take action the parents should take up the gauntlet to enforce the rule or offer punishment. What happens in your house is your responsibility but you must make a choice to accept the challenge.

GPS 4: Family Values

It is sometimes lonely being the head of a family where you choose the moral values to follow. An endless variety of influences tempt you and your children into breeching your values. For example, television can be a wonderful center of knowledge or a great wasteland devoted to undermining your family. There are now reality shows that include everything from teenage pregnancy to heavy-drinking playboys.

How do you overcome the influences that put such strain on your values? You do it with *vigilance*. Use the parental controls on the television and preview each program before you make it available for your child to view. Record programs to view before your child sees them. If there are moral lessons to learn or educational values, watch the prerecorded show with your child so you can share feelings about the action on the screen. Don't allow the outside influences to have the upper hand. Censor the shows with a click of the tuner.

Outside influences flood into the home through the Internet. These are still pioneer days for the World Wide Web and, like in the old West, there are few policemen. You need to police what your child views on screen. Spend time with your child, or at least in the same room, while they surf the net. If you allow them to have an email address, make sure you have the password.

One of the biggest mistakes many parents make is to allow their child to have a private computer in his or her room. Never use the Internet as a babysitter for younger children. When you consider some of the sites offered on the Internet, it's like hiring a babysitter with tattoos, a foul mouth and a propensity toward child molestation. These influences can speak louder to your children than you can and provide far more entertainment than you do. Don't let it happen.

Monitor the children with whom your child spends time. If you don't like the verbiage of a child when he or she visits your house, inform him or her of the rules. This stops negative influences in your home. If the visitor refuses to follow the rules, then he or she simply doesn't belong in your house, nor does your child belong in his or hers. If the foul-mouthed visitor follows your rules, allow him or her to stay but do not allow your child to visit his or her home since you have no control over the influences in that house.

The key is always involvement in your child's life. There is nothing wrong with checking your child's room for drugs, guns, and other harmful things. You are, after all, the parent. There are far too many negative influences in the world. You are the only one responsible for knowing your child's behavior. Only give your child the right of privacy when they earn it through their actions.

Teaching your child right from wrong and making them internally responsible for their actions can help you avoid strict and onerous enforcement. Start their lessons in responsibility early in life. If a child understands there's a price for every decision he or she makes, he or she will weigh their decisions far more carefully. Teach your child what is right and wrong and be firm and consistent with the consequences. Your child is human and as with all humans, imperfect. Love him or her as he or she is, but help him or her to be better.

GPS 5: Vital Links

No matter how loudly you speak, what you *do* speaks far louder. There are links between your words and actions that are either positive or negative. If you insist on honesty and then privately brag about lying on your tax form, what are your actions really saying?

There are links between the amount of time we spend with our children and the sincerity of our belief that they indeed are the most precious gifts we have. You can directly link lax parenting to rude and unruly behavior, or foul language to a passive parent who chooses to ignore the facts.

Children do not raise themselves. No matter how much you protest the actions of a teacher or school corporation, if you haven't provided the guidance at home to teach your child right from wrong, someone else has to do it. In yesteryear, if a child received punishment in school, the minute the parent found out, he received worse at home. Today, many parents bemoan the condition of the schools and yet are the first to complain if their child receives a bad grade or punishment. Do the words and the actions fit together? In many cases the answer shows there are no links between the two.

Do you speak out for more discipline in the school and then fail to provide it at home? The only action you can control is your own. Look closely at your home life and see if what you say links to what you do in the home. Look at the words of Joshua 24: 14-15 and decide if you've only verbally made a commitment and then failed to make the follow-through of behavior.

We all fall short, at one time or another, as parents. There are no instructions that come when you birth a child or first hold him or her in your arms. You simply have to rely on your own moral compass to find the best way to raise him or her. You will make mistakes, change your mind later on the wisdom of a decision, and hope to find better ways of doing something, but if you outline your values and determine the links to those values, the errors won't count.

If the children are learning less in school, work with them at home. If Bobby doesn't do his homework, take the time to sit and watch until he does. This is one way that action links your words to your beliefs. Taking time to know your child is another way of loving your child. You have no control over the behavior of others but you do have control over your own house. Assert that control so it links directly to your moral compass and family values.

Unless you have a plan of action that involves a deeper underlying value, *saying* something and *doing* something are two different things. Once you set your moral compass and decide what falls outside the boundaries, the rest is easy. What you believe, then, directly links to what you say, and you can give your family guidance it can follow that comes from the heart.

GPS 6: Influences

As long as today's busy parent runs around attempting to take advantage of every opportunity for the children or simply to make ends meet, something is lost. Dinner used to be a time for a family to get together and share views. Often many lessons were learned over the dinner table and values were passed to children at the same time. But in today's fragmented society, there's no time for family.

Judo, piano, voice lessons, volleyball, soccer and other outside activities often fill the child's day to the point where there simply isn't time for the family. Instead of a moral compass offered through the conversation of adults or interaction with the children, today's children receive their guidance through peers and media. The Internet and its easy access also bring a new dimension to family values plus new dangers.

It simply doesn't have to be that way. Once a parent looks closely at what he or she believes is important, he or she will toss aside extraneous activities that don't support these beliefs. This doesn't mean there should be no more soccer or piano. It simply means that you make choices, and within those choices make time for your child to interact with you—the parents and heads of the family.

Monitoring what your child watches on television and sees on the Internet is easier now that there are parental controls. You still have to take the initiative and set those controls. You and only you should decide whether your child spends time in front of a screen that shows lurid or violent pictures. This obligation is included in the job description of parenting.

Voting for state-sponsored censorship of literature, television and the Internet has *never* worked. Turning off the television, computer or not allowing specific books in the house has *always* worked.

If it takes a village to raise a child, then you're doing something wrong. You're relinquishing your rights as a parent and allowing others to feed your child their beliefs. Some parents have to work long hours to support their families, but that doesn't mean that they give up the right to be head of the family. The mission to provide a cohesive family unit may seem difficult. The fact is that *anything* that is worthwhile is difficult.

Look at the amount of time you spend talking with your children. Analyze what you teach your child with your actions. If your child isn't living up to his responsibilities, take an honest look at whether you've offered a good example. Do you make promises to your children you never intend to keep, but simply want to quiet their whining? What are you teaching them?

Know the friends of your children and spend time with them in your home. Do the friends follow your house rules while they're in your home? If not, do you tell them what the rules are and explain that if they aren't followed the child is not welcomed? It's tough but it also teaches everyone present that you have family values that you won't compromise.

Making certain there's time for your family to be together is one of the most important missions of your life as a parent. You cannot teach values if you have no pupil and children can't learn family values with an absentee parent. Set the standards for your house. Make a choice and live by your values.

GPS 7: The Village

In order to raise a child successfully today, you have to understand and acknowledge your moral values and ethics. Once you clearly define them, you have to find a way to enforce rules and maintain those values. However, if you depend on the rest of the neighbors to help you, as in "it takes a village," you also have to know whether their values are the same as yours.

Just like a successful family, a successful neighborhood-village requires interaction among the members. You can promote the interaction by visiting with neighbors. Simply dropping by the homes of those in your neighborhood and introducing yourself could initiate this. For those less adventurous, a friendly wave or self-introduction on a happenstance meeting can also start the dialogue. You don't have to ask them their deepest beliefs, but if you maintain an open conversation, you'll find out by the things they say.

Once you establish a good relationship with a few neighbors, let them know that if they see your children doing anything that is dangerous or that the neighbor knows you wouldn't want your child to do, they should let you know. You should further ask if, should you see a neighbor's child doing something that is dangerous or wrong, that neighbor would want to be told. If it is extremely dangerous, you should let your neighbor know that you would want them to intervene and alert you later. Ask if they want the same response from you. That way, it makes the intervention appear less judgmental and more helpful. This simple suggestion leaves the door open for the neighbor to help you as a second set of eyes. Most people don't want to "butt" in, but if given permission, want to help.

Even though you reach out to others, it doesn't mean you've

changed your values to reflect the popular idea of the day. At one time, permissive parental control, promoted by Dr. Benjamin Spock, was the hot new way to raise a child. That phase taught most people that children want boundaries and need a clear understanding of the rules of the road. Popular ideas and good moral judgment don't always mesh. Because of this, if the "village" ideals are not yours, you must maintain what you believe for your own house. Just make sure the rules of your path are just and fair.

Should you make your neighbor's business your own? That is a difficult question. Visiting a neighbor and showing compassion are all part of being human. If you see someone in trouble, sometimes all he or she needs is a friendly hand extended to help, a shoulder to cry on or someone to listen. Each year spousal abuse and child abuse occur because no one took the time to intervene. Most of the time, child abusers don't want to hurt their children but they have nowhere to turn to seek help. Providing an outlet or resource is the loving, neighborly thing to do.

Today's schools are part of the village. Your children spend half their waking hours at the school. In order to be proactive in raising your children, you must have a voice in the school. Most teachers welcome input and love parents who actively become involved in their children's education.

Teachers and administrators can't make the schools function smoothly without the help of outside influences such as parents. The schools will run and pupils will learn but not to the extent they do if the parents involve themselves in the activities both during school time and after school. While some parents may not be able to help directly with the school operation or functions due to work or lack of transportation, they can provide the much-needed support for the school at home. Making the child accountable for the lessons and homework, contacting teachers by phone to discuss the best method of helping the child and school, supporting the teachers and attending school board meetings are all ways a parent can help.

Neighborhood support comes from interaction and involvement. Many of the innovative and successful programs in the schools today first involved the parents but ultimately involved the whole neighborhood. Dialogue between the schools and parents helped establish programs to give parents requiring help an understanding of what they could do to improve the quality of their children's education. The open dialogue allowed parents to "own" the success of their children's education by allowing them a voice in it.

The recognition of the important role parents play in their children's education means that each person is responsible for what their child receives from the educational experience. If you choose not to take an active role but delegate the responsibility to another, you have no right to complain or criticize those who take affirmative action.

We are responsible for the habits we teach our children. If children attend school with an attitude of self-responsibility, they answer to their own consciences rather than wait for parents or teachers to punish or remind them to study. Rather than complain about the bad job the school does educating, a proactive parent digs in to see how he or she can help resolve the issue and turn it around. Your proactive actions also pass to your child. If you believe you're personally responsible for your family's future, your child develops that same understanding. If you believe that it's not your fault and others are responsible, he or she too will sit around and complain without ever taking hold of the reins that control his or her life.

It does take a village to raise healthy and well-educated children, but the village is not a geographical boundary. It is a collection of like-minded parents with the will to take charge of the education of their children and work with others toward that goal. There is only one answer to the crisis in education and it lies in each citizen, whether parent or otherwise. Changing the schools can't happen with the actions of one person, but one person can make a difference if they rally the support of others.

GPS 8: Education and Civil Rights

Many people claim that education is the civil rights issue of the 21st century. If you listened to the acceptance speech of Senator McCain at the 2008 Republican convention, you first heard that claim. He advocated choice in schools and included charter schools, private schools, and public schools from which parents could select. Since then, others have carried the gauntlet but no one seems to find the right way to do it.

As politicians look for the magic formula to make our schools better and our students smarter, money from Washington flows freely. We often view our educational system as we do our medical system and look for the magic pill, the magic bullet, the easy fix for a problem that is eroding our society in the same way a cancer consumes the body.

The statistics show that American education is in trouble. *One third* of all children in America don't make it to the graduation platform. The number of dropouts in poor neighborhoods increases to the fifty % mark. Many of our graduating students aren't prepared for college or the workforce. However, we continue down the same road, doing the same things and thinking that something will change. That is the definition of insanity, doing the same thing repeatedly and expecting different results. Instead of getting better, our schools are mired in swill and anger with shootings, lawsuits, and a further decline in the educational system.

Arne Duncan, U.S. Secretary of Education, reported to the National Conference of State Legislatures that because of the combination of lost revenue and public assistance, each high school dropout costs our nation $292,000. A report by the Bill and Melinda Gates Foundation noted that the economic output of our country would increase by $2.3 trillion if we improved the educational system. Unemployment is almost twice as high for dropouts as those with a high school degree and four times as high as it is for those who finish college.

Hardest-hit are the inner cities and urban areas, with minorities at greatest risk. Black children, on the average, are as much as three years behind in education as their white counterparts. It's a proven fact that once a student falls behind, he or she is at much greater risk to drop out of the system.

Not every minority child lags behind. Many minority students outperform their white counterparts and achieve more. The difference lies in the family unit. If parents accept nothing but the best from their child, the motivation to succeed often carries the child beyond the average despite economic conditions and family poverty.

Instead of becoming a statistic and wallowing in the self-pitying bath of the "have-not group," the active minority parent participates in the system, sometimes silent to the public eye, by ruthlessly accepting no excuse for poor marks and letting his or her child know that he is capable and expected to produce the best.

The most effective parent, regardless of creed or color, is the parent who becomes involved with the school while maintaining a strong, firm hand at home. While one person can make a difference, one person that unites the parents in the neighborhood can make a giant difference in the education of not only his or her child but the rest of those in the area.

According to Allan Golston, president of the Bill and Melinda Gates Foundation's US Program, not only does the teacher's perception of the student play a huge role in the achievement of the student, the student's perception of the teacher also plays a role. With this knowledge in mind, we have to look at the lawsuits aimed at the teachers and School Corporation and the attitude the parents instill in the students to see if there is any correlation between that and the achievement of the individual children.

What does a child hear when his parents blame the teacher for his poor marks, instead of holding him personally responsible for his actions? He hears that he can't learn because the teacher is ineffective and cannot teach him. The results, just like any other self-fulfilling prophecy, are that Johnny simply won't be able to learn, not because *he's* incapable but because he's been told the *teacher* is.

School administrators must welcome the help of the parents and not attempt to elevate themselves due to their educational status. Every parent has something to offer, regardless of his or her personal achievement. The schools cannot control the activity of the gangs but a group of dedicated parents can help prevent their children from joining and can even outnumber the gang members if they present a united front. The schools can help to build confidence in the student, but ultimately, the family and parents have far more control in that area.

Parents also need to listen to the schools and the teachers. By respecting the institution and the staff, they instill that respect into their children. Only by working together as partners can any change in the education system occur. They need each other and the exchange of ideas to succeed. The problem is too important to allow color or personal feelings stand in the way of the students' progress.

Besides the sense of self-responsibility, America has also lost the sense of accomplishment for a job well done. You see it in the faces of the store clerks and fast food servers and it reflects in the sloppy service of others in the work force. In our schools, the sense of accomplishment and completing a task, no matter how insignificant, with pride and all your effort, is no longer a virtue. Instead, we lower standards so that no one feels like a failure. In reality, by lowering the standards, the school is simply saying, "You are incapable of accomplishing this task to the best of your ability." We have created the generation of failures by accepting less than the best of our students.

Can this all be turned around? The answer lies in our future actions. Do we continue to throw money into an unsuccessful system or start using the resources found in the community? Are the parents in the poorer neighborhoods less capable of parenting—or have they been pushed out of the system? Do we need to educate the parents first before we can make any progress educating the students? These are all questions that must be answered before we can make any dramatic changes in our system. The war on poverty has been raging since the Johnson administration, and we're losing the battle. It is time for those in need to dig in and no longer accept pitiful handouts from the government but take charge of their lives and the lives of their children. The same holds true with the affluent parent. The family is the key to the educational crisis, and by refusing to turn their children's future over to the hands of the bureaucracy, doors will be unlocked.

GPS 9: Ethnicity and Race – African Americans

In our discussion in the next several chapters of the effects of ethnicity and race on education, we will examine educational issues through the lenses of these key indicators:

- Social Standing
- Lifestyle
- Economics
- Expected Outcomes
- Realities
- Roadblocks

We will also discuss changes required by society and by specific ethnic groups.

If they are from low-income backgrounds, African Americans have more to overcome in the traditional school setting. According to the U.S. Census 2008 report *Enrollment Status of the Population*, of all black youth aged 16 and 17, 5.8% were not enrolled in any secondary school. By contrast, of all white youth aged 16 and 17, 4.6% were not enrolled in any secondary school. This is a significant difference.

As Amy J. Orr reported in *Sociology of Education* in 2003, young black individuals from homes with a higher economic structure (wealth) tend to have the same advantages as their Caucasian counterparts. The keys are the family's belief system, the location of the school, and the importance placed on a good education.

Often in the underprivileged black neighborhoods, even the

language of the black student is dissimilar to that of white society. African Americans who use so-called Ebonics as their primary language in the neighborhood find themselves at a disadvantage when they enter the world of proper English. Even those with a college education who come from a poor background often have an accent indicating their heritage.

The key is the language and the desire to use proper English. Proper English simply isn't "cool" in lower economic black neighborhoods. In fact, you'll often hear young Caucasians using the language of poor blacks in an effort to become mainstream. The record industry promotes the language barrier with top rap and hip-hop songs that only those who speak Ebonics can understand.

Social Standing

The African American student is often in a crisis. If he decides to work within the educational system, other black students often ostracize him. If, however, he glorifies his ethnicity with the use of neighborhood language, he is a failure in the school system. In the past, this was less of a problem for other minorities immigrating to this nation. The groups' desire to fit into the American lifestyle often included learning proper English and speaking it without any inflection that might indicate their family history.

Because of the low pecking order in society, the African American community created their own pecking order in lower economic areas. In the inner city, gang members and drug dealers often are at the top of the economic ladder. They use Ebonics as their primary language. As the popularity of this type of language spreads, those who use it are at the top of the pecking order in the "hood" but often lack the skills necessary to function in the schools.

Lifestyle

As mentioned before, there is a wide difference between the higher economic black lifestyle and that of the African American in the lower economic bracket. Simple things like good nutrition become difficult in the inner city. While there are fast food restaurants galore, there are few if any grocery stores where the neighborhood people can purchase fresh fruits and vegetables. The heroes in a poverty-stricken African American neighborhood will often differ from those of the affluent black student. In many cases, gang leaders and drug dealers are the leaders and often role models in the lower economic areas, regardless of color.

Economics

The key to the dilemma of the under educated and failing African American is partially economics but also the expectation of failure. The ability to see a better way of life is often non-existent in the poverty-ruled household. Many parents simply abandon their belief in a better life and pass this defeatist attitude onto their children. The children in many lower economic neighborhoods see uneducated gang members with impressive cars and large amounts of cash. The need for a good education is not apparent and not valued.

Expected Outcomes

Unfortunately, unless there is a dramatic shift in the value system of many of the African American families in poor areas, there will be a continued stagnation of their position in society. Gangs and guns are a poor way to pull out of poverty but may be the only answer chosen if the disregard for the education system continues. High levels of crime and the vicious cycle of dominant gang leaders will also continue.

Realities

The African American student needs belief in not only the educational system but also their ability to work within the educational system. While the streets offer high peer pressure, parents in African American families are the key to making a difference. If the parents support education and firmly believe this is the way for their children, and use strict and consistent disciplinary action, then there is hope for their future. Unfortunately, hope and belief are often lacking when money is tight and there seems to be nothing better on the horizon.

Roadblocks

Well-intentioned government officials often believe that the answer to the African American dilemma in education is lowering standards and throwing money at the problem. The true answer is not to accept less from these students but request they live up to their potential. Graduating under performing students is one way the system glaringly states they have less potential to learn. A self-fulfilling prophecy then takes place and the scores for these types of students drop.

Changes Required by Society

We need to focus our attention on improving the neighborhood schools and involving parents in order to see any improvement in the educational scores for the African American student from an economically deprived area. Insisting on specific standards and extending a hand to get more parental involvement are all ways to help solve the problem.

Changes Required by African Americans

When it comes to education, the African American student and community need to focus more on the "I cans." The parents of the students need to enforce rules while encouraging their students to achieve more. This is the primary difference between lower economic African American families and those of means.

The problem does not stem from the *actual* inequities of society but the *belief* that they exist. Regardless of race, it is a far tougher journey from the jaws of poverty to the upper reaches of society, but with belief and perseverance, anything is possible. Valuing both education and the student's ability to achieve makes the difference between success and failure.

GPS 10: For Hispanic Americans

Similar to the African American student in economically deprived areas, Latinos often find themselves without hope and language skills to excel in the educational system. As reported in the U.S. Census Bureau's 2008 *Enrollment Status of the Population*, of all Hispanic youth aged 16 and 17, 6.2% are not enrolled in any secondary school, a dropout rate higher than for both blacks and whites.

Language may be a barrier. Often schools provide courses in English as a second language (ESL) but the students go home to speak only Spanish, their native tongue. This frequently negates the day's education in their new country's language.

Social Standing

In lower economic areas, race and ethnicity play a far more important part in the pecking order than they do in areas where the families live comfortably. Lower economic whites often believe themselves to be superior to both black and Latino students. African Americans see the newer group, the Latinos, also as an inferior. They frequently place in the bottom of the pecking order in these types of situations.

Lifestyle

Often the lifestyle of the Latino family dictates the outcome in the classroom. Since in closely-knit families there is no need for a second language, they frequently maintain their ethnicity and fail to learn English. Unlike previous immigrants to America that spoke only English in an effort to fit in, many Latino families choose not to fit in but create their own culture area within the cities.

Economics

Just like Caucasian or African American students, the economic situation is the deciding factor. Students from homes of higher economic stature show very little differences in their academic abilities. However, the same is not true of those with lower incomes. Often there is no communication with the schools since the parents speak no English and are intimidated by the meetings. Expectations are often lower and jobs available to the group pay less. If the family is illegal, this difference is even more distinct.

Expected Outcomes

Because of the illegal status of many Latino families and the lack of desire to learn the English language, the gap between the Caucasian, African American and Latino student will continue.

One additional roadblock is the dependence on government assistance. While receiving help in a time of trouble and job loss, many families find themselves quite comfortable learning to use the "system" and depend upon it for their income. Welfare is one way that keeps the Latinos from achieving success in school. If there is no necessity for a better job, there is no drive to attain it.

Realities

According to U.S. Census Bureau statistics, in the year 2008 only 68.4% of Latinos between 25 and 29 had a high school diploma. In the same year for the same age group, African Americans showed 86.6% high school diploma rates with non-Latino whites showing a 90.5% rate.

While the rate for Latino college graduates was at 10% in 1975 and did not increase in the year 2000, African American students went from an 11% rate to an 18% rate in the year 2000. Non-Latino whites increased from 23% in 1975 to 34% in the year 2000. Other educational statistics show there is a large and growing gap between the races.

Roadblocks

One of the biggest roadblocks to success is the value placed on education in the Latino community. The first indication of the lack of educational incentive is the decision made by many new Latino residents to forego learning English and continue to speak their native tongue. There are studies done in the past that show children from non-English speaking households that live in the United States fare far worse in the educational system.

Changes Required by Society

As a society, the United States caters to those that choose not to speak the designated language of the country, and therefore aids in defeating the Latino children in striving for academic success. Schools, stores, and places of industry offer interpreters or bilingual instructions. This reduces the necessity of speaking any other language but the native tongue.

Regardless of nationality, strict adherence to performance levels needs to be enforced. Insisting on English-only instructions in all facets of life is another way to encourage those who have no skills to learn the language.

Requiring all citizens to speak English can only be accomplished with proactive measures. Since sponsorship programs are one method of attaining entry into the country, each immigrant should have an automatic interpreter until they learn the language, saving the government money to devote to more pressing issues. Opening the schools in the evening to adult classes in English is one method of helping those without skills in the language.

Changes Required by Hispanic Americans

The previous immigrants to this country initially had difficult times but integrated into the system, often within the first generation. Strict adhesion to the English-only rule and the desire to seek a quality education were the factors that allowed the quick economic and educational growth of those people. Today, many times in the Latino family, this is not true.

In order to excel, the entire family has to work with the system and promote the importance of a good education. Parents need to learn English, just as their children must, so they can participate as parents in the system and help their children if problems arise. Attending evening school or learning English on their own gives the student a role model after which they can pattern themselves. What the student learns at home, in most cases, and the attitudes they carry are what make the difference between success and failure in the schools. If there is ever to be equity in education in the Latino community, Latino parents need to understand the important role they play in their child's attainment of a degree and must stand up to the plate to help.

GPS 11: For Asian Americans

Asian students excel in the school system today. According to recent numbers, even though Asian Americans make up only 4% of the population, they account for almost 20% of the students fortunate enough to attend prestigious Ivy League schools. The U.S. Census Bureau reports that in 2008, of all 21-year-old Asian Americans, 97.2% held a high school diploma. While there isn't a basic difference in original test scores, the Asian student simply seems to perform better.

Social Standing

The social standing of the Asian student varies greatly. Rather than only the race of the individual, social standing depends on the country of origination, the length of time in the United States, and the family income. After the war in Vietnam, many Vietnamese orphans found homes with U.S. families. Even though they physically appear to be of Asian descent, they are just as "American" as their adoptive parents are.

These Asian students may even have a higher social standing because of their exotic appearance. The same is true for today's students whose parents came with the other 200,000 Vietnamese and Cambodian refuges between 1975 and 1979.

Language barriers and lack of knowledge of local customs block many of the new immigrants from Asian countries from gaining high rank on the pecking order. The highest population of Asian immigrants into the schools comes from China, followed by the Philippines, India, Vietnam and South Korea. Again, if the student comes from a well to do family and has honed skills in English, they often end up as leaders of the pack.

Lifestyle

Regardless of the economic conditions of the family, in most cases, Asian American families believe in delayed gratification. They often stress practical aspects of living and words of wisdom. While happiness is important in the Asian American culture, the belief in education and economic freedom is also at the top of the ladder. When 15-year-old girls responded to a question about their expectations for college graduation, 58% of the white teens thought they would graduate. The number jumped 85% when discussing the topic with Korean and Japanese teens and exploded to 95% when Indian teenagers responded. The parents put education far above outside activities and made certain they knew what their student was learning in the classrooms so they could help at home.

Economics

While there are great differences in the economic levels of Asian American families, eventually those Asian families with a heritage of hard work, frugal lifestyle and delayed gratification tend to become the higher achievers. The country of origin does play a role in this but only to the extent of the values the family brings with them. Like Joshua of the Old Testament, this has more to do with the discipline emoted by the family head.

Expected Outcomes

Asian students tend to surpass other groups in their educational achievements. Asian families place high value on good academic records and self-discipline. When school ends for the average student, frequently the student from an Asian family finds it continues at home. The number of college students from Asian backgrounds continues to rise, as do their test scores. The U.S. Census Bureau reports that in 2008, of all Asian young people aged 20 and 21, fully 81.1% were enrolled in college. In contrast, the rate for all groups was 48.5%.

Realities

The Asian country of origin makes a big difference in the expected outcome. However, on SAT results, Asian, Asian American or Pacific Islanders far surpassed all other ethnic groups including white Americans. The trend for higher achievement will continue, unless a dramatic change occurs or the belief system of the Asian family changes.

Roadblocks

For the family that exerts parental control over its children and leads an actively involved life with the parents as the family head, the only roadblock will be maintaining that tradition. The Americanization of the family that allows the children to have control would lower the gain for the Asian student. There is a discrepancy between Asian islanders, Chinese, and Indian Asian students. Frequently the strong family culture of the Chinese and Indian families eliminates the roadblocks based on language and economics.

Changes Required by Society

The Asian group shows that the family involvement in the student's educational process makes a world of difference in the outcome. In the book *Top of the Class: How Asian Parents Raise*

High Achievers and How You Can Too by Soo Kin Abbound and Jane Kim, daughters of Korean immigrants and high achievers, they explain the strict lifestyle of the Asian family and how it helped them become a surgeon and attorney, respectively. Society needs to emulate the family values of the high achieving Asian student.

Changes Required by Asian American Families

Because of the discrepancy among the Asian subgroups, the best answer is simply to maintain the values placed on discipline and high achievement for those that have it and adopt those values if they didn't come with the culture. While Americanization is encouraged, adopting all cultural beliefs would be a mistake for the Asian groups that excel.

The biggest obstacle to overcome for this group is the language barrier for the newly immigrated. If the educational scores are low for a group due to lack of English speaking abilities, it behooves the entire family to learn the language so they can help the children achieve in school. Participation in school functions by parents is also important and often neglected if the parent feels inadequate. As with any group, insistence on high academic achievement and self-responsibility resonates as the primary way parents of any race can help their children.

GPS 12: For Caucasian Americans

Caucasian students have always outscored most groups on SAT scores and all groups in general on school achievement tests. They are going to college in increasing numbers; the U.S. Census Bureau reports that in 2008, 50% of white students aged 20 and 21 were enrolled in college, as opposed to 36.8% of blacks and 29% of Hispanics. This doesn't tell the entire story since the race of a student is only part of the picture. There are discrepancies within the class of students of European background.

Social Standing

The white student has normally felt the comfort of being at the top of the chart in the area of social standing. Sometimes this is not the case, however, in areas where heavy populations of other ethnic groups exist. Just as in any endeavor in life for popularity, numbers do count.

Lifestyle

The lifestyle varies greatly, primarily based on economics. The poor white does not have a lifestyle even close to the affluent white or suburban white. Instead, the poor white family tends to live much as any poor black, Hispanic or Native American family. As with the black and Hispanic family, a large divergence in lifestyle exists between the economically deprived and those who live comfortably.

While the lifestyle of the suburban student overflows with extra curricular activities and parents focused on school, the poor urban and rural whites do not have the same advantages. In these cases, the advancement through education is frequently not a family value. In some cases, this exists because the potential of achieving the dream seems too distant.

Economics

The average Caucasian family has a higher economic standard of life than the average black, Asian, or Hispanic family. The results of the 2008 United States Census show that of general population living in poverty, only 8.6% of them were non-Hispanic white, while 11.8% were of Asian background, 23.2 % were Hispanic, and 24.7 % were African American.

Expected Outcomes

The discipline of the Asian family frequently is not part of the Euro-white American family. Often parents allow the children to control the household through the constant demands of the extracurricular activities of the suburban family. Rather than taking charge of the children's education by involvement with the school, focus on self-discipline and attention to the curriculum, many Caucasian parents voice opinions rather than take action to get involved. In poverty-ridden areas, parents often feel inadequate to participate in the educational system, and therefore their child falls behind. The continuation of too-few disciplinary actions at home and lack of involvement will cause the Caucasian student to continue a downslide on test scores.

Realities

The Caucasian student scored the second best of all U.S. ethnic groups on SAT scores. However, lack of discipline in the school and at home produces children with limited self-discipline and sense of self-responsibility. This unfortunate oversight of the parenting public to instill the virtue of self-responsibility also robs the child of the ability to move higher in education and feel the power of achievement through effort.

Roadblocks

American popular culture is a significant roadblock to the education of its children. When important discoveries in space fade from the news because we are focused on the antics of a drunken celebrity, our country is in trouble. The school population in general can repeat all the words of a complicated rap song but struggle to answer the question, "How many states are there in the United States?"

Poverty and lack of belief are roadblocks faced by all poor ethnic groups. Students from a lower socio-economic standing show a 10% lower test score than those of a higher standing. This occurs regardless of parental involvement. Some of it may come from stress or lack of access to valuable resources.

Changes Required by Society

Classrooms filled with unruly children and teachers bound with lack of power are the true roadblocks to a better education. Parents suing school corporations for disciplinary actions received by their students, and other parents suing for poor educational results only leave the entire system in a rapidly declining state. Whether white, black, or other ethnicity, parents and students alike need to take responsibility for success or failure in the school. Government measures to lower requirements and the granting of judgments against the schools for doing their job need to stop. Until we demand academic excellence from students regardless of race or economic standing, Caucasian students and all American students will find themselves lower on the world educational ladder.

Changes Required by Caucasians

Taking charge of your own life is the key to success. Without that ability, the individual becomes a pawn to the whims of others. Without belief that the efforts of the individual count, that parents are truly the leaders of the home, and that education matters, there will continue to be a downslide in our educational system.

GPS 13: For Native Americans

When it comes to SAT scores, Native American students are ahead of their Hispanic and black counterparts but still lag dramatically behind the Caucasian and Asian students. Because of the ability to isolate the Native American student, due to the existence of reservation schools, numerous studies show positive results for increasing the educational scores of the Native American.

Social Standing

Amazingly, the standing of the Native American student is higher in areas where there are limited students of that background. Being Native American is popular in those areas. However, nearer reservations, the social standing of the Native American drops in proportion to the population, a reversal of what is normal. Some studies show that using programs that includes curriculum based on the traditional Native American culture raises the overall scores of academic achievement. Perhaps this has to do with the societal standing and the self-image of the student.

Lifestyle

The lifestyle of the Native American varies by economic factors and location, and depends upon the tribal nation and whether the Native American lives on a reservation. Those living on reservations historically found themselves surrounded by substance abuse and poverty. However, not every Native American reservation is the same. Some tribal leaders took up the gauntlet to improve the lot of their nation. Business opportunities have increased because of the actions.

Many tribes now have their own educational programs and tribe-sponsored schools. In the case of the Cherokee nation, they have a government that the United States recognizes as a nation. It has three governing bodies just as the U.S. government does and has made great advancements for its people.

Economics

For centuries, the Native American suffered from harsh economic conditions. The United States government forced them onto reservations; many years later, however, some of the tribes found there were oil reserves on the land or other economic possibilities such as casino operations. Overall, even though the great Native American nations are on the rise, many still suffer from drastic economic conditions.

Expected Outcomes

Since many of the Native American nations are taking charge of their own educational system and reservation schools are using newer techniques that combine the heritage with the educational environment, the Native American student show signs of dramatic growth. Several studies have shown the achievement gap between white students and Native Americans becomes non-existent when it involves a focus on the culture and culturally sensitive training plus cooperative learning experiences. Programs that united the parents and schools also improved test scores. The outlook for the Native American is a positive one.

Realities

The reality for the Native American student is that he or she will often have to leave the reservation in order to find higher paying jobs. Even though there have been dramatic strides by the nations to improve economic conditions, aside from casinos there are few opportunities for higher income employment. However, the tribes taking charge for the future of their constituents has made a difference in not only the education of the children but also the future economic development of the tribe. Not all Native Americans, however, are part of the improved change.

Roadblocks

The traditional educational process seems to be the biggest roadblock to the success of the Native American student. When schools instituted programs including culturally based material and used teaching methods such as outdoor classes for science, the students excelled and testing revealed similar scores as Caucasians. Programs that involved the family with the schools also raised the scores of the students. The roadblock in this case seems to be the tendency for some Native Americans to allow others to dictate the operation of the schools and curriculum.

Changes Required by Society

Some of the most insightful beliefs of the Native American culture are important for our society. For instance, the traditional belief that destroying the land insults one's ancestors is a wise means of teaching conservation. That it is important and wise for a person to listen carefully to a speaker, think deeply about what they are saying and then formulate a response, is another Native belief that would benefit all Americans. Introducing culturally based education and cultural pride into reservation curriculum is just one step in the improvement of the education for Native Americans.

Changes Required by Native Americans

Three important conclusions come from recent studies on the educational process of Native Americans.

1. When the tribal leaders take charge of their own futures, including using culturally based education, the tribes and the educational systems benefit.

2. Involvement of the family with the schools enhances the educational development of the student.

3. The improvement of self-esteem through either cultural methods or parental involvement comes from both of these and makes a huge difference in the advancement of the student.

The Native American nations need to look to themselves to make improvements for their future generations.

GPS 14: For Other Minority Ethnic and Religious Groups

America is a melting pot of many countries, religions and races. While many studies show the results of tests for "others," they fail to identify the groups included in this. This group could be broken down not by nation but by religious preference such as Jewish or Muslim. However, all we know is that they are "other" and rank fourth in the SAT scores, lower than Asians, Native Americans, and Caucasians but higher than African Americans and Hispanics. In order to understand what other means, you have to know who is included in the group.

Social Standing

While we are a melting pot, we aren't always a "happy melt." There are always groups shunned because of their differences. At this writing, Muslim children often feel the sting of the difference due to the attack on our nation September 11, 2001. Other groups such as Puerto Ricans often feel the sting of bias in the school, primarily due to the high number of the population in lower economic situations and educational levels.

Economics

Again, in most cases, the economic condition of the family plays the most vital role in the advancement of the child. Next to parental involvement, it is the highest factor in the success of the student. Of course, in many cases, higher socioeconomic standing also represents higher parental involvement. Frequently those parents with poverty issues either must work to make ends meet and therefore have limited time for school involvement or feel inadequate to become involved.

Expected Outcomes

Tightly knit groups such as traditional Muslims often shun the educational process of the West and use parochial schools to teach their traditions in addition to supplying the necessary education. Because these traditions are often strict, many times the students leave the schools far more prepared than others in public schools. In the rules for these schools there is no room for student involvement with drugs, sex, guns, and alcohol. While the rules are sometimes broken, as with any school, the strictness provides a framework where better educational outcomes are expected.

For poverty-ridden groups with loose family ties, the prospects are not as cheerful. Instead of learning new ways to pull their group up, often the families of these pocketed poverty groups look to government assistance. If a parent suggested that the child needed to better himself or herself with an education, they would be condemning the life they lead. This ironic cycle is the Catch-22 for many impoverished groups.

Realities

The cycle of poverty-begetting-poverty is one of the realities of life. Until those imprisoned by the grasp of lack of education and economic resources understand the situation doesn't have to exist and can be changed by their own motivation, there will be no climb to the top.

Parochial schools for specific religions, particularly those of Islam, may not provide the quality of education desired. As with most parochial schools, often funding is low, with teachers being either dedicated members of the religion or those who can't find a higher paying job. The focus on the importance of the religion often detracts from the education provided. However, there is far more structure in these types of schools, with less time spent on disciplinary action.

Roadblocks

The biggest roadblock to the group may be the size of the individual subsets in the group. Because this group is a combination of small minorities, each subset is a very tiny portion of the population. For those of Muslim persuasion, the bias of some American people creates huge problems for the students. Those who keep strict adherence to the Islam faith find their differences are often tradeoffs between either keeping the faith or getting an education.

Changes Required by Society

A breakdown of the subgroups into specific ethnic origins would be the first and most important job to identify the problems within the groups. While the score for this "Other" group is relatively high, it is an average. Indeed, it may be an average for each subset but also could be an average that contains one subset with a very high score and several with low scores. This muddies the water when it comes to solving the educational problems of the individual groups.

Changes Required by Minority Religious and Ethnic Groups

If the educational scores are low for a group due to lack of English speaking abilities, it behooves the entire family to learn the language so they can help the children achieve in school. Participation in school functions by parents is also important and often neglected if the parent feels inadequate. As with any group, insistence on high academic achievement and self-responsibility resonates as the primary way parents of any race can help their children.

Part Two:
Taking Action

GPS 15: Is Education an Entitlement?

The Race to the Top federal grant program is part of the American Recovery and Reinvestment Act of 2009. It's one of the largest reforms involving education-directed discretionary funds in U.S. history. The primary goals for the program revolve around four specific areas.

The first is to adopt specific standards for public schools and a way to assess the preparation of the students so they have success in the workplace, college, and the world economy.

The second is to build a data system that accurately measures the growth of students and areas of success. The hope is that the information gleaned from the system will help teachers improve instruction.

The third goal is for states to find ways to reward the good teachers and principals and find methods to recruit them and retain them.

The last goal is for the states to transform underperforming schools into higher achieving schools.

For the winning schools that both applied for the program and achieved these goals, there are awards of discretionary cash. In these times of economic stress, the prize looks particularly tempting to many states that are facing financial shortfalls and need the additional boost.

For the U.S. Department of Education, the hope is that one of the states will find the magic bullet that, when applied to school districts across the country, will miraculously cure all the ills of the school corporations.

The problem is that the magic bullet doesn't lie in innovative techniques but in society itself.

Schools must operate in a societal environment that is not always supportive. Once the pinnacle of educational excellence, in the past few decades U.S. schools have found their authority to be challenged. In the classroom, teachers no longer have the final say. Often the voice of the parents and students speak louder than the teacher's. Personal responsibility is no longer viable and measuring up to standards is deemed to be outdated. Busing to improve the education of all children has hurt the learning environment of those that need educational aid the most by removing them from close proximity to a neighborhood school and stressing an already overstretched school budget.

Race to the Top is another attempt to reinvent the wheel and do it by throwing cash at the problem. The states, of course, aren't going to let this opportunity for increasing income go past and want to participate. Just like many past programs, cash doesn't solve the problems intertwined with our society. Society and the attitude toward learning must change.

Rather than offering a competitive grant award as Race to the Top does, a close examination of the schools in other countries would be a more appropriate place to start.

Finland would be one country that the American educational system could emulate. Instead of the students starting school at age five, they start at age seven. The students all enter a government-funded early childhood program that does not focus on reading and math but on social behavior and knowing one's self. This may be the reason that the Finnish students show a high level of personal responsibility for both life and their education. In our country, we hold the educators and educational system accountable for teaching the curriculum but in Finland, the *students* are accountable for *learning* instead. This is very different from what we see in schools today.

Unlike American schools, Finnish schools don't put everyone

on a college curriculum program but divide the students for the last three years into vocation training and college preparedness, with 53% going to college. Their dropout rate is substantially below that of the United States.

In fairness, American schools face significant problems not shared by the Finnish schools. In the U.S., approximately 15% of the school population does not speak English when entering. Even though it isn't politically correct, the government needs to address this issue by making all services English only, giving incentive to learning the language and relieving the schools of the burden they face.

On a world level, education is a privilege, but most people in America believe it is a right. Although the government mandates the attendance of school until a specific age, that makes it no less a privilege. In many other countries, there are no schools for students to attend. Many of these children are hungry to learn and yet have none of the fruits of education on which to feast as we do in the United States. Yet, students in the U.S., faced with a veritable buffet of learning, often choose to opt out of the system and waste the life-sustaining opportunity available to them.

One of the biggest problems in our country and educational system is the fact that it's readily available. Nobody appreciates the gift because of this. Other countries view our dropout rate and feeling of entitlement with great disdain. We chose to abuse our system with lawsuits, undisciplined children, and general disregard for the concept of self-responsibility, and yet we scream when Johnny can't read. We claim that it's the fault of the teacher and the educational system and we, as parents, or Johnny, have no part in the outcome.

While the concept of discretionary money and the use of it going back to the states' own needs is important and a big improvement over nationally mandated changes, there are far better ways to solve the problem. We need to go back to basics. Our country has a myriad of educational grants, programs and requirements. These overlap or negate each other. Instead of another program, someone needs to stop and wipe the slate clean. They need to begin from scratch and look at the most important part of what helps a child to learn.

That missing piece is *personal responsibility for education*. Rather than a collage of programs, some that extend far beyond the framework and simply don't fit, the development of one program on which to focus our resources is far sounder.

GPS 16: Rights and Responsibilities

You don't have to be born in America to feel entitled to the systematic receipt of the bounty of benefits. Our government has made it clear that every child who is old enough for an education is entitled to one. While the concept is important, the lengths the government takes to insure this to every child—including those not born in the U.S. and those who don't speak English—is beyond rational logic.

The right to an education should not include the right to that education in any language, but only in English. Instead of insisting the minority learn the language of the majority, the government insists on providing services of teachers and materials in the native language of the child. This places undo burdens on the school systems and the taxpayer. The cost to the taxpayers for both illegal aliens and children born in the U.S. to illegals is astronomical.

California, a state with one of the highest budgets for the education of illegal aliens and children of illegal mothers, spent more than $7.7 billion in the 2004/2005 school year for the services necessary to provide for their education. The state had a $6 billion shortfall in their budget that would not have existed had they not had to provide the additional services. It also could provide more equipment and teachers for the school or even lower the property tax base.

This brings us back to the question of *privilege* or *right*. While the effects of this particular group are easy to assign a cost, what about the wayward student who simply wants to join a gang or disrupt classes? Should you continuously give that student the second, third, or fourth chance to cause chaos in the classroom?

The topic does not have an easy solution. It is, however, something to discuss at home. You don't have to talk about the situation with illegal aliens or mention future gang bangers. You should, however, note the high cost of education and make note that every citizen who pays taxes, particularly property taxes, pays for that education and that the cost of the "free" education is not free.

When you make your child aware of this, make certain you include that he or she owes it to society to do well in school so he or she can give back as an adult.

Too frequently parents focus on the rights of individuals without any mention of the responsibilities that come with those rights. If education is indeed a right, not a privilege, your children and your family have some responsibilities to fulfill. The state or local schools need to identify those responsibilities and require the students to fulfill them.

However, this is America, and our schools have very little power to require anything of the student. In this case, you as a parent must take action to do so, if only for your own house.

If every parent made his or her child accountable for the child's own actions, the schools would no longer be in the state of chaos that exists today. With the right to an education, there comes the responsibility to ensure the rights of others to receive that same education. If a child is unruly, he or she destroys the rights of others by creating on obstacle on the path to that education.

With the right of an education comes the responsibility of fulfilling the requirements of that education. Any child who fails to study for examinations, or do homework or other school assignments, is not fulfilling the responsibility that goes with that right. You cannot change the behavior of other families but you can insist that in your house, your family keeps the implied promise to do that.

Look upon education as a privilege. If it is a privilege, then to whom is the privilege afforded and can the schools withdraw the privilege? Why don't we represent education as such, with the schools given the ability to pick their students, honoring only those who show perseverance and promise?

We have become a nation where the phrase "give me because I exist" is the watchword of the day. We feel we are entitled to all things American, including education, with no expectation of returning anything for them. Adherence to the rules is no longer fashionable. If someone makes a mistake, we assert, it should not count against him or her, even though that mistake may cause harm to others. The schools fill each year with children who want everything handed to them on a platter and parents that back their attitude of entitlement.

You may believe that every child deserves a good education, and within limits he or she does—but there is a price to pay for everything.

The backbone of tomorrow's nation attends the schools of today. If we raise children in the attitude that they deserve everything without the labor that goes into the necessary work to achieve or close attention to the rules, we will never prepare them for the journey as an adult.

Not every child deserves an education but every child deserves the *opportunity* to receive one.

The semantics of this sentence make the difference. By neglecting rules—even rules about the legal citizenship or classroom behavior—and catering to those who break the rules in an effort to make sure the child gets the education we offer, are we not then teaching a lesson that has a lasting effect on the children? Instituting the attitude of responsibility to the school, the classroom, the academic material, and the laws of the land gives every child the opportunity if he or she chooses to accept the responsibility.

GPS 17: Family Discussions

Joshua Interrupted

While Joshua stood fast and told others to choose their way of life, it isn't that easy for parents today. Communication in today's world is far more intricate and invasive than it was in the time of Joshua. No matter how fast you stand on an issue, or try to raise your children in a specific mindset, or voice your opinion on the operation of schools, society and peer pressure always have their say in the final product, the adult child. This makes the role of the family even more important.

Conflict is everywhere. Today the schools attempt to teach every point of view, with the end result that no one is happy. Even the mention of Biblical verses such as Joshua 24:15-16 bring parents screaming to board meetings in protest of religion in the schools. Even though the story is one of leadership and the freedom of choice, it comes from the Bible and court rulings prohibit it.

Yet, other examples of curricula which are not endorsed by all parents are more than acceptable to society.

The freedom of choice has always been an American virtue held holy and close to the heart. The right to select a religion or not select one was one that the forefathers held dearly. Many of the families that came to this country left their homeland to avoid religious persecution and made sure the Constitution included the right to practice any religion without interference from the state. It was indeed following the Biblical words of Joshua, saying-by-saying "In God We Trust" but you may embrace any religion you choose.

Today, that freedom falls by the wayside. It is no longer that way.

The Santa Rosa, Florida, School Corporation, after a threatened suit by the ACLU representing atheist students, signed a Consent Agreement, which the courts accepted. The decree forbids school officials from "promoting, advancing, endorsing, participating in, or causing Prayers" and from "orally express[ing] personal religious beliefs to students during or in conjunction with instructional time or a School Event."

As reported by Liberty Counsel, Denise Gibson, a Santa Rosa elementary teacher for twenty years, said in testimony that the order forced her to tell parents she could not respond if they talked about church or their faith. She could not even respond to an email from a parent if it contained a Scripture verse or "God bless you."

Santa Rosa County School District clerk Michelle Winkler testified that in fear of violating the consent decree, she had to hide behind a closet door to pray with a co-worker who sought comfort after losing her two-year-old child. Because of the agreement, the ACLU sued one teacher for having her husband pray in her stead at a private gathering. Two members of the staff faced charges and arrest for praying at a private event.

The courts eventually deemed the Consent Agreement unconstitutional but not before the teachers and many of the students faced retribution.

Can you raise your family with moral values in a setting where simple prayer to a god of your choice no longer is viewed with tolerance? Today's world is upside down and doing so is difficult but not impossible.

However, the right to select your own religion and method of worship is not the only snag in the goal of uniting your own house first and taking a family position on issues.

The first problem is the right for children to select their

viewpoint. Small children normally follow the beliefs of their parents because they lack any knowledge to debate it.

Teens, however, are a different matter. Teens tend to think independently and often in opposition to their parents. Is it right to force them into accepting a family view?

This is one place that a family meeting night can help unite the family rather than divide it. Discussing issues openly and calmly can help clear up misconceptions of both parents and children on hotly debated subjects. Immigration reform, gay marriage, war, racism, political ethics, as well as other timely and hotly debated issues can be part of the family night discussion.

Uniting the family is only a small part of the family meeting. Clearing the air, gathering facts, and openly talking about issues without threat of retribution can help the rebellious teen become a logical thinking adult. During discussions, however, you have to be prepared with facts, or your family meeting will fall apart. Getting the best information possible and as much of it as you can doesn't hurt anyone and only improves the fact-gathering ability of children and adults alike.

Make no mistake—there may be challenges to a family night open discussion. Some issues don't have facts attached to them that support a view, or the facts are based on disputed Biblical references, such as gay marriage. The proposed Cordoba Initiative that contains a mosque to be built at Ground Zero is one of those. It's a "feeling" issue rather than a tough fact debate. Even though the governor of New York offered viable parcels of land a little further away from Ground Zero, the builders of the center were offended and refused. Is this a freedom of religion issue, an attempt to find a prime location for commercial purposes, or simply a kick in the face for Americans?

By openly discussing hot issues such as this, you may find your family more divided than united. Does the family night then become a threat to cohesiveness or should the children feel comfortable airing their views and the family agree to disagree in a compatible manner? Dissention occurs whether we discuss issues or not. Is it better to have them out in the open rather than bottled up waiting for an inopportune moment for them to surface? You must ask yourself those questions before you begin the process.

Issues on immigration and political corruption have more fact-based arguments but also an emotional side. No matter what your feelings on the issues, your child might feel differently. If you support open immigration, your child might have a differing view based on experiences in school. The same is true if you support tighter laws against illegal immigration. It is hard to stand firm against illegals if your child's best friend is one.

You may never solve all the problems of the world by having open discussions within the family but you will let your moral, political, and ethical values be known to the family. While chaos may reign and the rest of the world take opposition, if you firmly believe a specific way, you have not only the right but also the duty to express that belief at home and share it with your family.

In the days when everyone sat around the dinner table and talked, formal meetings were never necessary. Values and concepts were shared. Today, with children busily attending classes and after-school functions, there is little time for a family dinner. A meeting night may be the only way to achieve passing on your beliefs to your child. You don't have to insist your opinions are right for everyone and perhaps shouldn't. You do, however, have to let the child know what they are and back your beliefs with as many facts as possible. Without giving your child a road map to life, you'll find they're liable to end life's journey in a bad neighborhood filled with dangers and corruption.

GPS 18: Education Is Empowerment

In order for any individual to succeed in this world, education is necessary. Having an education brings empowerment to the individual. It also provides freedom of choice. After all, not every employer offers acceptable pay. These days, it takes a lot more than just minimum wage to earn a living.

Most people without proper knowledge are struggling just to survive. They're on food stamps, Medicaid, and depend upon other forms of government assistance. A lot of individuals make so little that they cannot afford basic necessities. They are in debt and without empowerment. Those without an education struggle and bounce from job to job until they choose to go back to school and take courses in something that interests them.

Most careers require that you have some sort of skill acquired from a technical college or university. Careers that require a certificate, associate degree, or bachelor's degree include accounting, computers, nursing, cosmetology, welding, HVAC, teaching, marketing, and dozens more. Those that require advanced degrees include medicine, law, and architecture. Having training provides the advantage. It also leads to higher pay, thus leading to even more empowerment.

People have the choice to go back and continue their education at anytime, which is sometimes what makes it so difficult. Assuming that you have all the time in the world is a huge mistake. The sooner you go back to school, the sooner you can start living the life you deserve.

Obtaining an education is a *choice*. There are no excuses. If you have children, put them in daycare. Everyone deserves his or her own piece of the pie. Getting out and taking advantage of what is being offered to you not only benefits you, but society at large. If more people took advantage of the system and claimed what was rightfully theirs, there would be less debt, less poverty, and less crime. The government is especially kind to individuals who are on a low income, providing even more available assistance.

Empowerment from education also leads to higher self-confidence. It expands the mind and opens the doors of the imagination to even more possibilities. While you were working at your dead-end job, all you could think about was how you were going to get your power bill paid for the month. Will you even have enough money for groceries? What about your car payment? Or, will you ever have enough money to even purchase another car? If you do, it will likely be an old clunker. This is the way of life for a person with no education. This is the way it will always be. It's as if the individual is locked inside of a dark box full of problems, worries, and struggles.

Money should not be the primary reason for seeking this type of empowerment, however. The main reason why a person should achieve an education is to obtain a life of free will and his or her own decisions. Everything you want is already yours, especially when it comes to knowledge. Simply think of something that makes you happy in life, and make a career out of it. Before you do that, you must learn the skills necessary.

Many people worry about whether or not they will be able to afford an education. There should be absolutely no worries when it comes to finances because there are loans, grants, scholarships, and other forms of financial aid available. In the United States there are many programs available to assist nearly anyone in getting the education they need. An education ultimately belongs to anyone who wants it.

GPS 19: The Three Key Empowered Players

In today's education system, parents, students, and teachers are the three key agents for change.

Parents

Many parents feel they don't have enough background or information to make a difference in their child's educational process. Many parents sometimes feel left out of the most important part of their child's day—the school experience. However, by seeking the knowledge to help them feel more comfortable, they will truly become empowered, because *knowledge is power.*

What are some of the requisites for gaining that empowerment? These ten action items can help you to become more involved in your child's educational process and the quality of education he or she receives.

1. Read the school letters your child brings home or go to the school's website to gather information, particularly if your child is lax about notices. You'll find a wealth of information, from afterschool activities to school lunches.

2. Attend meetings that involve the PTA. These meetings will help you get a feel for parental involvement in the school. By listening to the praise or concerns of other parents, you'll also get a general feeling for both continuous problems in the school and areas of excellence.

3. Go to the meetings scheduled with your child's teacher. This is by far the most important way of gleaning information about your child's education. A parent/teacher conference is for input from the teacher and the parent. Often either the parent or the teacher discovers issues that exist and eliminates them through simple communication.

4. Attend school open houses. Of course, your prime concern is to go to your child's room, but you'll gain extra knowledge if you view the exhibits of all the classrooms in the building. The material that decorates the walls and desks often gives an insight into the entire educational program of the school.

5. Find out when the school board meets and go to the meetings. By law they must be open to the public. Often people attend budget meetings but dismiss the other school board meetings as unimportant. You can offer your opinion when the board brings up topics that will have a lasting effect on the school. Introducing information before the board makes a ruling can prevent many hours of argument to reverse it.

6. Learn what's new on the educational front. The Internet offers an abundance of information on schools that excel in education. Look for programs where you can be instrumental in improving your child's school.

7. Learn about national tutoring or mentoring programs where businesses allow employees to donate an hour a week to tutoring or mentor children. These programs often relieve the teaching staff and support staff. They provide extra attention to the children who need it.

8. Hunt for ways to get the community involved in the school activities. Community outreach programs through

the schools are one way to get community involvement. The more the community is involved with the schools, the less alienated they feel when property taxes increase.

9. Examine the budget and look for grants. If you're more of a numbers person, you'll feel at home looking at the school budget and finding ways to cut expenses. Bring your talents to the table and let the board know your findings. Finding government and private grants for the school can bring empowerment for you, the teachers and the community.

10. Listen to your children. While most parents brush off information after a long day, listening about a child's day is one way to glean important information and make the child know that what happens in school is important. If you hear the same concerns day after day, check them out. If, on the other hand, your child reports delight and joy in their school day, write a thank-you note to the teacher and send a copy to the school board. People often take time to complain but seldom take time to praise.

The true story below gives one reason that parents must become empowered:

In an affluent community, two high school seniors were vying for the coveted honor of being the class valedictorian. The young man had a grade point average of 97. The young woman had an average of 96.5. Even though she had a lower grade point average, the young woman was granted the honor. Why?

During his four-year course of study, the young man failed to take a class that was listed as a part of the criteria to hold the award. Because they did not know of this caveat to achieve the high honor, the young man's parents were outraged.

Another twist to the story is that the parent of the young

woman worked at the high school. Clearly the young woman was made aware of the requirements to be class valedictorian and she strove for this high honor. You would think that a guidance counselor or someone should have given the young man the information or saw to it that he took the proper classes to assure him being able to compete for the top honor.

Teachers

No matter how much teachers believe in the rule that knowledge is power, they often forget it when it comes to their own personal empowerment on the job. Of course, they know the ABCs and basics of education—that's what the school board pays them to teach. However, learning ways to make the system better and empower themselves is seldom a topic taught in college.

If you're one of the frustrated teachers in today's classrooms, you don't have to accept being on the bottom of the totem pole. Only by claiming your true power can you be the most efficient teacher you're capable of being. Many people learn in their youth to be humble and empowering yourself doesn't have to clash with that belief. Empowerment gives you the inner strength to stand for your convictions without raising a voice or being pretentious.

Here are the ten most important action steps you need to take.

1. Listen to the parents. Often teachers want to show the parents that they know the child and the material. In doing so, they frequently fail to ask the parent for input. While the child often spends more waking hours with you during the school week, the parent has known them for a lot longer and has insight into their home experiences.

2. Call the parents when a child performs well. It's a simple task but one that's quite effective. If you keep in contact with pleasant surprises, you'll develop a trusting

relationship with the parents and one that is beneficial to helping the child. This gives you more validity in the eyes of the parents and empowers you.

3. Attend community functions. If you don't live in the district where you teach, make certain you go to functions where you'll see your students and/or parents. Developing relationships is an important part of empowerment.

4. Stand up for your beliefs. If you believe you need to retain a child and the parents take the issue to the school board, attend the meeting. However, request that the permanent record state that the promotion of the child was due to parental insistence and administrative decision. You eliminate any possibilities of later retribution because "Johnny can't read," and maintain your standing as a professional.

5. Find the most effective ways of classroom discipline. If the classroom is out of control, no one learns. Learn methods that keep your voice level down and still keep the children under control. Two of the biggest issues in today's schools are the lack of discipline and the inability of the teacher to enforce the rules. Find the methods that fit your class and personality, and don't deviate.

6. Take an active interest in the school board meetings. As an insider, you'll often see places where the board could allocate funds for an improved educational environment. Occasionally, the board doesn't have the inside information to make critical decisions. If you're uncomfortable speaking out at board meetings to correct erroneous information, talk to a board member privately after the meeting to give the information.

7. Learn about the educational systems of other countries

that have better results than the United States. You'll probably find some programs that transfer well to your school. The more you know about what works, the more you have a chance to change the system.

8. Find grants online that fit your curriculum. The government and corporate and private foundations offer grants to schools and teachers with innovative ideas. You can save your school money and make your dream classroom come true.

9. Follow through with action when you say something. It doesn't have to be disciplinary in action; it might be something as simple as saying the children will have a five-minute break. No matter what you say, make sure you're willing to follow through. Your word must be reliable or your credibility is gone.

10. Relax and take time to enjoy life. Learning relaxation techniques for the end of the day and doing them can keep you teaching longer, more effectively and healthier. In order to be the best, treat yourself as if you were the best, and take time for you.

Students

Students often feel that the school is a dangerous place emotionally. While unfortunately there can be physical dangers in the schools today, you can eliminate many of the emotional landmines by empowering yourself. You don't have to be stuck-up (in fact, that hurts more than it helps); you simply have to learn how to function in the schools. Knowledge is power and empowerment can help you not only in school but also later in life.

Here are your top ten action items.

1. When you're a student, knowledge is power in more than one way. Of course, the first way is the classroom knowledge. The more you learn in class the more likely you'll have a positive school experience.

2. Remember that school is your job. While you aren't seeing money for schoolwork, it's the basis for your future income. Sometimes you'll believe there is no purpose to the subject you're learning and yet years later the information will be useful. Approach each lesson and class as though it were important to your future.

3. Take responsibility for your actions. Nobody wants to get in trouble but if you've done something wrong or failed to do your homework, accept the consequences. Honesty to yourself and to the world empowers you far more than anything else you can do.

4. Right along with taking responsibility is avoiding the blame game. No matter what the circumstances, if you have a problem, you're most likely part of the cause. If you're not learning because you don't understand the material, talk to the teacher. If the teacher won't listen, talk to your parents.

5. Present a pleasant demeanor and friendly outreach to everyone. Frequently, the school has a pecking order. You'll be tempted to pick on those below you and feel the pressure from those socially above your position. Don't participate. Treat everyone with respect and ignore the pecking order. Normally, when you don't retaliate or react, it stops. If you find you're harassed even when you ignore the harassers, don't handle it yourself. Tell an adult.

6. Participate in activities at the school. There are many

clubs and organizations that improve the school and help you make friends or learn valuable skills. The more you learn, the easier it is in school. Extracurricular activities are not only fun, they're also ways to meet people and empower yourself with new skills.

7. Help other children who have problems learning. Many schools offer programs where older children tutor younger ones in various subjects. Get involved. You'll feel better about yourself and that's part of empowerment.

8. Find ways to improve the school. Everyone sees problems but few come up with solutions. Look for solutions and ways to help rather than just complaining. If the school is a dump, start a movement to clean it. If the classes are out of control, ban together with like-minded students to help reestablish class control.

9. Check out national contests. Often there are competitions that your school might participate in but nobody knows about them. Look for these competitions—often with generous prizes for the school—and see if you can find one that is right for your school.

10. Become part of the solution rather than part of the problem. True empowerment means you are in control of your own actions. If you become a problem solver, rather than part of the problem, you'll have far more control. The good news is that this skill is also quite valuable as an adult and you can get an early start on developing the skill.

GPS 20: Advocates on Call

No matter what the government program, there is one thing normally lacking. It is *personalization*.

Too frequently, people are lost in the shuffle of paperwork. They become names and numbers with no faces and no control over their lives or the paths that the system takes them on. The person seeking to better his or her life often gets caught up in red tape and quits because he or she feels as though no one cares. The heads of programs begin to see the individuals enrolled as statistics with the same problem.

They aren't just statistics. Each individual has something different that blocks him or her from achieving his or her full potential. Each one needs personal treatment and help from someone familiar with their situation.

Every school district should have a program staffed with people who can be Advocates on Call, ready when needed to carry the water for the vulnerable, the weak, and those without knowledge.

An advocate is an individual who follows the recipient of the service as long as necessary. At the same time the advocate is advocating, he/she is teaching the "how-to" to parents and leveling the playing field. Advocates on Call would be an educational aid that would not take the place of parenting but supplement it. It would not only teach the parents how to navigate the stormy seas but also help them recognize the opportunities available for their children.

Students and parents often find themselves intimidated by the red tape that chokes school administrations. This intimidation often causes them to turn and run from what could be a life changing experience. The Advocates on Call could be their 911-call-center for help. Such a program could help the recipient overcome that fear by supplying not only support but also knowledge of the process.

In the long term, Advocates on Call will *save* money. While there are many programs that offer financial assistance to those academically, physically or emotionally challenged, they simply create a dependency upon the program rather than create an independent entity empowered with knowledge. Dependent users keep drawing upon the resources of the system, and the expenses grow. Advocates on Call breaks this cycle of dependency.

Advocates would be trained in workshops, providing important knowledge to help the advocate give the recipient a head start and some self-confidence.

There would be practical benefits. If the parents work or are unable to attend any of the meetings with their child, such as Individual School Plans (ISPs), the advocate would go in their stead and share the knowledge of the meeting. The same would be true of disciplinary meetings at the school or teacher conferences. The advocate would become part of the team that creates the bridge between parents or recipients of the service and the rest of the service providers, including the school.

If you've ever filled out a government form, you understand how vague the instructions can be. Imagine attempting this with little education and few reading skills. Simply looking at the form becomes daunting. The advocate can help the recipient through this and any other problems they face. Generically, Advocates on Call can be useful for all services recipients—disabled, veterans, seniors, and all users of government services.

Advocates on Call would be an individualized program offering the participant and family one familiar face throughout the educational process. It would be an individual not involved in deciding whether a child or individual passes or fails, gets a job or doesn't, but one that becomes the friend of the downtrodden who can offer solid advice to change lives and help people achieve their maximum potential.

GPS 21: Anger Management

Today's schools can be dangerous. Gangs pose a threat in almost every inner city school. The rural areas aren't free from the potential of violence; just as in the inner city, there are sometimes children who can no longer take the pressure of peer teasing or have relationship problems when it comes to the rest of the school population. These children see the resolution of anger on television programs or at home, and the resolution they see often ends with a gun or other act of violence. The headlines often bear witness to these seemingly random acts that cause so much pain and national grieving.

Anger blocks effective learning. Besides being a danger to the children, anger is a poisonous toxin to the person who bears it, whether they act on it or not.

Frequently, anger comes from feeling inadequate. This builds into a powerful ball of passion that rots the inside of the child and later the adult he or she is to become. It is the shadow of a cloud blocking the absorption of all that is good in life. This includes not just friendship and interaction but also learning.

Today more than ever, children need to learn how to deal with anger. They need to learn self-discipline to control not only anger but also the rest of their lives. It is too late to wait until the child enters high school to give that training. By that point, many of the traits are already in place and the damage is done.

Many other countries focus on learning self-responsibility before learning the ABCs. We need to take heed and consider this type of program for our early learners.

Anger management is nothing more than taking the

responsibility for your own feelings. When taught at an early age, it takes the form of learning to take responsibility for one's actions and feelings. Since many of the useless acts of violence occur because of teasing or shunning by peers, this type of training could help prevent that from occurring. The early training gives the pupil an understanding of not only the effect of their actions on others but a sense of self-worth. That sense of self-worth can stop the teasing and ostracization of other individuals and give each pupil the self-confidence to ignore the taunts.

Too frequently, students learn angry behavior at home. This can be transferred to the schools. No matter how valid the school program is, if the home environment negates the effects, it is useless. In practice, the school should be required to alert the parents when their child acts out in the school. If the behavior continues—suggesting a deep-rooted cause—it would be wise to offer the parents training in anger management. While the anger management program for parents should not be mandatory or presented as a way of pointing a finger, it could be offered to the parents as a supplement, to help them understand the training their child receives so they can help them accomplish the goals at home. Parents already angry at the world don't need another person accusing them of bad parenting.

Through the constant attention given to self-responsibility and anger management, the school will not only become safer, it will open the student to the mindset optimal for learning. By involving parents and giving them some of the training so they can help their students, it can provide relief from domestic violence that also takes place once the students leave the schools.

GPS 22: Vocational Work Study

In order to make our schools great again, we need to consider *all* jobs as important, not just college degreed positions. In Europe, retail clerks are specially trained for their position. They are professional. The fact that there are no unimportant positions in the world is a lost concept in the American schools. If every student learned to take pride in their work, regardless of their job, our country and the students would benefit.

We give great importance to the idea of a college education, only to find many of the graduates unable to find a position in their field of study. Filling the need for qualified workers does not always mean they require a college degree. It simply may mean they need to have the training and a helping hand to learn the position.

While we consider jobs in fast food restaurants, mall stores, and other retail outlets to be inconsequential, they often are the positions that make the difference between using the services of the stores and finding another place to purchase merchandise or food. It would be wise for private industry to fund vocational training centers to help provide well-trained employees for their businesses.

Too many high school students lack basic retail skills. The simple act of counting change back to a customer is a lost art. If there's no cash register to designate the amount of change the customer receives, often the worker is left frozen without a clue how to proceed. Simple tasks and instructions often fail to register to some employees. Knowing that six items are equal to a half dozen, or that if the bill is $5.10 and the customer hands you a ten dollar bill and a dime you simply give the customer $5 back, are frequently skills our new entries to the workforce do not possess.

Retail businesses such as home improvement stores would benefit from having individuals trained in the use of the various materials, tools, or items in the store. It is quite scary for the customer uninitiated in home repair to realize they know more than the clerk who is helping them. The student also could benefit by having a job ready and receiving more training on the job once they can work.

Why do students drop out of school? The college-bound students aren't the ones who suddenly decide they don't want to attend school. The dropout rate increases each year because students who require vocational training are lost in a sea of rhetoric and information that simply won't help them get a job. Career training at a center could help fill this gap and also supply those lost souls with a direction in life.

Industry would be wise to help begin the initiative and start programs that work with the schools to provide training and jobs for those who simply don't want, or don't qualify for, a college preparation course. The benefits received by the franchise, school and students would be massive. Besides lowering the dropout rate and providing jobs for those who have taken the program and have developed the necessary skills, a program provided by private industry affiliated with a designated community center/ entity would empower students and families.

The pride of the first paycheck at an early age sets the stage for future accomplishments. It provides a map to a better life for the student. Rather than looking for a way to receive a government stipend the student has a concrete position and way of earning an income.

The businesses providing the training would have better workers than they ever dreamed possible, trained in their way of doing business.

GPS 23: Schools on Flex Time

One way to solve the overcrowding of schools is to reconfigure the school schedule into a flex one which would allow for smaller classes at any given time period.

Move the high-performing students into a distance learning program in a room in the school monitored by a student teacher. High-performing students become independent learners, supported by limited formal teaching other than the distance learning monitors, and/or set up an interactive experience in which they participate through questions and answers.

Utilize other options to include peer teaching, peer tutoring, peer mentoring, and professional mentoring.

Adjust the school year so that classrooms and facilities are used year 'round, and not locked up and empty for three months out of every year as they are now.

Not in our lifetime will there be enough charter schools and/or private school experiences to provide learning for all children. They will never totally take the place of public education. It is time to reconfigure public education to meet the need of the learners. If smaller is better, then schedules need to accommodate this. Those who can be independent need to be independent, while those who need help need to have the personal attention they require.

Why not? Does every student need to have a teacher at hand? Can't other options be used to meet the needs?

GPS 24: Tutoring and Mentoring

Repetition, repetition, repetition was the way the early pioneers taught the ABCs and mathematics. Of course, today we have far more advanced techniques that use all the senses to stimulate the previously unused brainwaves of the students. However, it all comes back to one thing: repetition, but in a different manner.

But there must be more. Scientific studies have shown that children learn differently from one another. Some use the visual sense far more than the auditory. Others use tactile senses or movement to learn. However, no matter what way a child learns, extra positive attention from an adult, whether it is in the child's learning style or not, always facilitates the learning experience.

Tutoring is one method of not only increasing the amount of repetition for a child but also providing some positive feedback in a one-on-one situation. The tutor has the ability to teach the same subject matter as the teacher but with the individual attention, trying it in different ways until the child grasps the concept. When parents, frustrated with their child's progress in school, look for alternatives to help their children learn, they turn to private educational services such as Sylvan Learning, Veritas Tutors, Kaplan Test Prep, and Kumon Math & Reading Centers.

When Johnny can't read, private educational centers fill the void. These centers use a small ratio of two to three students per "teacher" to facilitate the child's reading. They use small modules of learning that take about fifteen minutes for the student to read and another fifteen for them to answer questions about the reading material. Nothing in the center is different from the material offered in schools except for the interaction between the child and the teacher. There is more individual attention and because of this the child's reading or math improves. The franchise owners as well as the teachers all believe this method works because of its past history. This belief combined with the power of individual attention makes it work.

Of course, there are fees. The cost to tutor one child at a place like Sylvan Learning Center can easily reach thousands of dollars. Most established learning centers offer a refund of tuition paid if the child's grades do not improve. Unfortunately, this does not help people of low income. While many of these centers offer some scholarships, there is not enough to cover all the needs. The centers have to remain profitable to keep their doors open, so that's understandable.

Many government programs offer title money to provide classroom aides that function in the same or similar manner to the commercial learning centers teachers. While the aide doesn't have the training the learning center teacher has, they do provide the same attention and often use the same material. The use of teacher's aides or teacher assistants often helps the slower-learning student but there is no title money for students who function at average or above average.

Should the schools provide extra help to every child or just the ones who are failing? On the level of fairness, it would seem that each child deserves special attention. However, looking at budgetary means, there simply isn't enough money in the coffers to do that.

There are alternative solutions for this dilemma. One solution is the mentoring programs offered by organizations including Mentor, the National Mentoring Partnership, and Big Brothers Big Sisters. These programs may only provide mentoring to a select group or may simply offer the services of private citizens to anyone who wants a mentor.

Programs such as National Mentoring Center involve business and the individual. Businesses allow employees to take paid time from the job to go to the schools and help any child who either needs it or signs up for a mentor, depending on the program. Simply, the mentor-employee goes to the school where he or she gives one hour of undivided attention to the student. Often lifelong friendships come from these types of programs because of the bond formed in that short hour every week.

Individuals sometimes volunteer in the schools for mentoring. Unlike the programs offered through businesses, these people receive no pay for their time away from work. These mentors also find the effort to be rewarding and form close relationships with the students, often giving them not only an educational boost but also life lessons as well. Seniors are often part of the rise in the mentor programs, which builds a bridge across the wide age gap of the student and the mentor.

If you have a child in school, you don't have to wait for an official program or outside source to find a mentor for your child. You have one in your own home. If every parent blocked out an hour every week on his or her schedule and devoted it exclusively to mentoring his or her child, the level of educational ability would rise dramatically. Often parents look to outside resources to find help for their children when help is standing at their own kitchen sink or sitting in their own living room. Special attention from an adult and a focus on the lessons is valuable no matter what the source, but particularly valuable when it comes from a parent, grandparent, aunt, uncle or other beloved relative.

No matter how advanced your child is, the extra time with him or her improves not only his or her scores in school but your relationship, his or her self-esteem, and his or her attitude toward education. If you feel that the process is important enough for you to schedule that time, the message transfers to him or her.

Just as the mentor from the business sector or volunteer mentor carves out one hour from the week without deviation, the parent or relative who mentors a child has to place as much importance on that appointment for the mentoring to be effective.

Every child deserves a good education but too frequently parents, and Americans in general, feel that it must come from an outside source, cost additional funds, or only come from those with a higher level of education. Once we decide to take back the education of our children and become actively involved we will find that love and positive attention helps fill many educational gaps for students of all abilities.

GPS 25: Faith-Based Initiatives

Increasingly, the federal government recognizes that many families rely on faith-based education. Whether it is simply a stricter environment, the involvement of the family, or more attention paid to self-responsibility, faith-based initiatives are now receiving greater attention. Parents are choosing schools and programs that focus more on the family, religion, and morals than the public schools, and these factors prove to be important in the final assessment of the student's progress.

In addition, federal Title 34, adopted in 2006, implements "executive branch policy that, within the framework of constitutional church-state guidelines, religiously affiliated (or 'faith-based') organizations should be able to compete on an equal footing with other organizations for funding by the U.S. Department of Education." This mandate cleared the way for faith-based organizations to apply for federal grants for programs that do not promote religious belief.

The Department of Health and Human Services has the Center for Faith-Based and Community Initiatives. The Partnership Center leads the department's efforts to build and support partnerships with faith-based and community organizations in order to better serve individuals, families and communities in need. While the Center exists to supply information and resources, it is important to note that it offers no faith-based funding. Rather, the Center "works to enable community and faith-based organizations to partner with the government through both non-fiduciary and fiduciary partnerships to achieve the goals of HHS and the specific goals put forward by the president for the Faith-based and Neighborhood Partnership Initiative."

What role do faith-based education organizations play? In lower income neighborhoods, part of the problem with public education is lack of involvement of the parents. Sometimes this occurs because of busing to distant schools where parents have limited access or ability to become involved. Other times it is simply a matter of intimidation. In many cases, the parents in these neighborhoods feel more closely tied with the church and are not put off by the religious component a faith-based school brings.

Other reasons that faith-based schools help in economically deprived areas are the same for higher income areas.

The first is the stricter adherence to rules and regulations. In faith-based schools, the school has far more ability to take disciplinary action. Because they aren't required to accept every student, simply the threat of expulsion from the school can make both parents and students take note of the rules and abide by them.

The second reason is the belief of the person sending his or her child to faith-based schools. Many of the parents want the same beliefs passed to their children. These religious beliefs often have to do with obedience and reverence, in addition to the responsibilities of human beings. Those underlying beliefs create an atmosphere conducive to learning.

Faith-based schools frequently don't have the financial resources that other schools have. This means that the pay scale for the teachers is normally far below that of the public school educator. However, a study in 1997 by the Partnership for Research on Religion and At-Risk Youth, an arm of P/PV, Public/Private Ventures, a Philadelphia-based agency in the forefront of demonstrating the work of faith-based and community organizations in civil society, investigated the success of faith-based schools. They found that in some of the most successful schools for at-risk children, the teachers sometimes went without pay for several months to keep the tuition cost down for students and schools open. This would indicate that the level of dedication was far higher and meant more to the end results than pay that might attract more professionals with higher qualifications. Of course, this is a luxury not every teacher can afford.

The 1997 study took place in Washington, D.C. and involved only the schools in the toughest area of town. The faith-based schools they studied showed the students attained high levels of basic literacy. Some of this was because of special attention to the individual needs of the children. Because these are primarily neighborhood schools, there was no busing and sometimes the children and teachers stayed as late as 7:00 pm or arrived as early as 7:00 am.

One difference between the attitude of many public schools and those in the ones studied was the potential for the students to attend college. The principal of Our Lady of Perpetual Help, Sister Elizabeth, told the interviewers that the reason they had such a high college enrollment for their children normally considered at risk for high school dropout is that they simply expected every child to go to college. With that expectation, they formed the foundation for the self-fulfilling prophecy.

At these schools, however, parental involvement was not a factor in making the school successful. In fact, it was similar to that of the public schools. The difference came from the staff of the school. The Sacred Heart Catholic School, located in the Adams Morgan/Mt. Pleasant neighborhood, a predominantly Latino area, showed that the positive reinforcement at the school may be the reason their children have an increased literacy rate. The school encourages the children to be not only creative but to nurture others to do their best. This environment promotes a higher level of excitement toward learning.

If these faith-based schools in an area known for school dropouts and illiteracy can succeed without parental involvement, just imagine if they also had the funds to educate the parents in the importance of their involvement to the child's ultimate success. The Texas Alliance School Initiative (TASI) partnered with the El Paso Interreligious Sponsoring Organization (EPISO) and showed that doing that increased the potential for learning.

The study used two sample schools: the Sombra del Norte Middle School and Mountain Vista Elementary. These schools are traditionally 95% Latino. Over 70% of the students were of families considered economically deprived. However, through concerted effort, the two groups increased parental participation, leadership, advocacy skills, and self-confidence. They used family education and parent leadership training held at parent academies and centers to do this. Even though the study was on public schools and the involvement of EPISO caused concern about separation of church and state, most parents became more involved in their school's decisions, which studies show results in higher academic achievement.

No matter what the religion, the moral principles and dedication shown in the faith-based classroom have proven to help in the education of children. Deeper involvement in the educational process by parents is a plus, and while it's not always part of the religious school program, with proper funding could become a major factor. In areas where religious schools reflect the beliefs of the neighborhood, the two combine well to produce well-educated individuals who might find themselves left to the side of the road if put in a public school environment.

No child has ever perished or been blocked by learning that "Thou shalt not kill" and the introduction of rules of living is more than just a cornerstone of the Judeo/Christian religions. It is the backbone of all religions. For those who wish to have morals taught in addition to self-responsibility and the "three Rs," a religious-based school might be just the answer. Additional funding for these types of schools could be one of the answers to our crisis in America's educational system.

GPS 26: Due Diligence

When it comes to the educational system's funding, one has to ask who's watching the henhouse. Higher costs with lower results should make you not only scratch your head in wonder, but also find yourself disturbed and attempting to find the answer. Every year there's a new educational initiative that costs millions of dollars and is the answer to all our prayers. However, the level of achievement continues to drop even though we throw more money at the problem. Are we approaching this like the bad parent who purchases more items for his or her children in order to get them to behave, rather than taking action to change the behavior?

Something is innately rotten in the state of our schools. It has passed the level of slightly smelly and now ventures into the land of nauseating. We have dropped from a leader in the world of education to one that can barely make it into the top ten, and depending on the type of criteria used, may not even do that.

According to statistics from the U.S. Census Bureau, during the 2007-08 school year the State of New York paid more per capita for public elementary and secondary education than almost any other state–$15,273, a whopping 67% more than the average state expenditure of $10,209. Yet despite spending vast sums it has a higher dropout rate than its neighboring New England states including New Jersey ($14,824 spent per student), Connecticut ($13,370), Massachusetts ($12,492), and Delaware ($13,283).

Obviously, from the study, a higher quality of education does not necessarily come from more money paid to feed the system. In fairness, unlike states with a higher rural population, one problem faced by New York is the presence of gangs and the related violence that comes with them. The majority of the cost of the educational system in New York was for staffing. Staffing can include extra funds going to teachers who choose to teach in the rougher inner city schools and the addition of security guards in the schools. All this adds to the extra expense. But just like inner-city schools in other areas, such as Chicago, often the priorities of the bureaucrats to address issues such as racial balancing, rather than focus on the student, add to the expense and detract from the quality of education.

When it comes to education, foxes in high paid positions guard the henhouse. In an effort to cut costs, rather than focus on waste or higher levels of income enjoyed by the administrators, schools in financial trouble first lay off important but low-paid service personnel. Just like other governmental organizations, the schools are not without bureaucracy. Much of the funding for schools goes to teachers and administrators with no ability to adjust for quality due to unions or airtight contracts. The very same people who develop and approve the budget are often those paid the most in the school system.

Making a difference in the schools has become an impossibility for many teachers. Tools and teaching techniques that were free and at one time proved invaluable have no place in our schools today. A hug or touch of approval as well as the ability to stop a child from causing harm by use of physical intervention, has no place in today's "enlightened" classroom because of the potential for a lawsuit from the parents. Yet these tools were often the most used in the classrooms when America was at its best in the area of education.

We reward students and their parents for illegal behavior. We not only allow those who break the law by entering the country illegally to receive a quality education but we also pay an extra price to have the materials available in a variety of languages and supply higher-cost teachers who speak those languages. The cost of providing those services to legal immigrants was never part of the educational system in the past. In the past, children and adults alike learned English and were proud to speak it as new citizens. The lifting of this new burden on the educational funds for the benefit of a few could rescue the system or at least make a dramatic difference.

While it is difficult to function in a system where you don't know the language, in the past immigrants from around the world made it their business to learn English. That is because there was no other way. These people flourished as a result and helped to create the great nation we once had. Today there is no incentive and the drain on resources strains the budgets of the American school system. One method of providing services to non-English speakers so they can better function in our society would be to remove all the duplication in material provided in various languages, take the English as a second language classes out of the school, and remove other "aids" to non-English-speaking children. Instead, the government could provide abundant evening and early evening classes with its own budget to facilitate both parents and students in learning the language. With this in place, not only would it reduce the budget of the schools but also reduce the need for other "aids" required for non-English-speaking parents.

Could any of these problems be tackled and progress take place? Sadly, the answer may be "no." We are too entrenched in political correctness ever to change the way the schools discipline the students. The country is too entrenched in lawsuits as an answer to problems (or the way to make a quick buck) to allow teachers to touch the children in any manner. Political fat cats control the pocketbook strings and often the public has no say in the method of spending. Finally, we have learned to coddle those who don't speak English rather than to encourage the use of the language and help them achieve the same greatness that previous immigrants found on our shores.

Of course, individuals joined together in a united goal to improve not only the school system but the nation as well could address each of these problems. By attending school board meetings and active participation in political and school decisions, one person can make a difference. The uniting of people with logic and common sense is the only way we'll find ourselves slowly rising from the mire we created.

GPS 27: How Teachers Can Get Parents Involved

Because of your close daily contact with your students, you, the teacher, may know more about an individual child's aptitude and behavior than the child's parents know.

Teachers need to remember that while the teacher knows the child's behavior in school and academic accomplishments, the parent has great insight into the child's home behavior and habits. Rather than create a competition of who knows the child best, the answer is to combine the knowledge and provide a united front. Teachers can help do this by recognizing the importance of the parents and using their wealth of information about their child and the child's social and home environment.

Studies show that the more involved the parents become in the educational process the better the process will be. Children with parents who make school visits and participate in school activities tend to do better in school because they also see that their parents recognize the importance of the education.

Teachers express woe about the lack of parental involvement, but unfortunately often do nothing to encourage it. In fact, by failing to reach out, teachers and administrators can discourage parents from participating in the educational process.

How do teachers begin? *Make contact with the parents.* It's that simple.

Of course, some parents are so used to hearing bad reports from the schools that they develop an aversion to anything school related. In cases such as those, the process is longer but the results are far more rewarding. Teachers should start with finding the *good* things the child does and then letting the parent know. If Jimmy is a handful but one day, quite out of character, does something nice for a schoolmate, let Jimmy know how proud you are. As soon as possible, march to the nearest phone and call Jimmy's parents to let them know how proud their son made you.

If Mary Beth seldom answers in class, but on one particular day has the solution to a problem, phone, write or stop over in person to let the parents know the accomplishment. At first, they'll not believe that was the reason you called or stopped by but if you leave immediately and don't say anything else, they'll begin to change their view of the school and Mary Beth's educational process.

When you hold parent-teacher conferences, always make certain that you use phrases such as, "How we can work together," "I need your help," "I have your child for eight hours but you've had them for eight years," and, "What do you feel is the problem." Let your children's parents know they have valuable insight and information on the child that you could use. Everyone wants to help and feel important so acknowledging that importance can bring parents to the school as allies and present an opportunity to form a united front toward helping the child in school.

Some parents feel they have nothing to offer. Just like your students, you have to help them gain the self-confidence to work with the schools and you to make a difference. Self-esteem does not come out of thin air—it runs in families. In reality, the more important that parent feels, the better he or she can parent and bring a feeling of importance to the child.

Single-parent families are often the most difficult to include in the school. Often these parents not only function as both mom and dad, but also carry one or two full-time jobs to make ends meet. For these parents, you have to make some allowances. If they can't meet traditional times, find times when they can.

Many parents, particularly in poorer neighborhoods, don't

want you to visit and see how they have to live. Instead of offering a home visit, offer a Saturday morning cup of coffee at a coffee shop or restaurant close to their home. It prevents them from rejecting the offer because of worry about their home, it provides a comfortable atmosphere for a conversation, and is really far safer than going into the home of someone you barely know. Make sure to tell them you'll call when you arrive at the restaurant and give them your cell number to call if they can't make it.

Sometimes the parent will stand you up with no notice. That happens and you've done your part. If he or she does show up, you'll often find a parent who truly wants to be part of the process but can't find a way. Help his or her and keep his or her in the loop with calls and notes. Find the best time to contact the parent in the future. Schedule a regular appointment every quarter.

Listen to the parent. Even if you don't believe one of their ideas will work, hear him or her out and see if the basic concept is good but the details need some reorganization. Parents are a valuable source of knowledge and information. Each one has skills that you can use to enhance the education of the students. Look to the parents as a valuable resource and you'll find that your children will excel.

Part Three:
What Shall We Do?

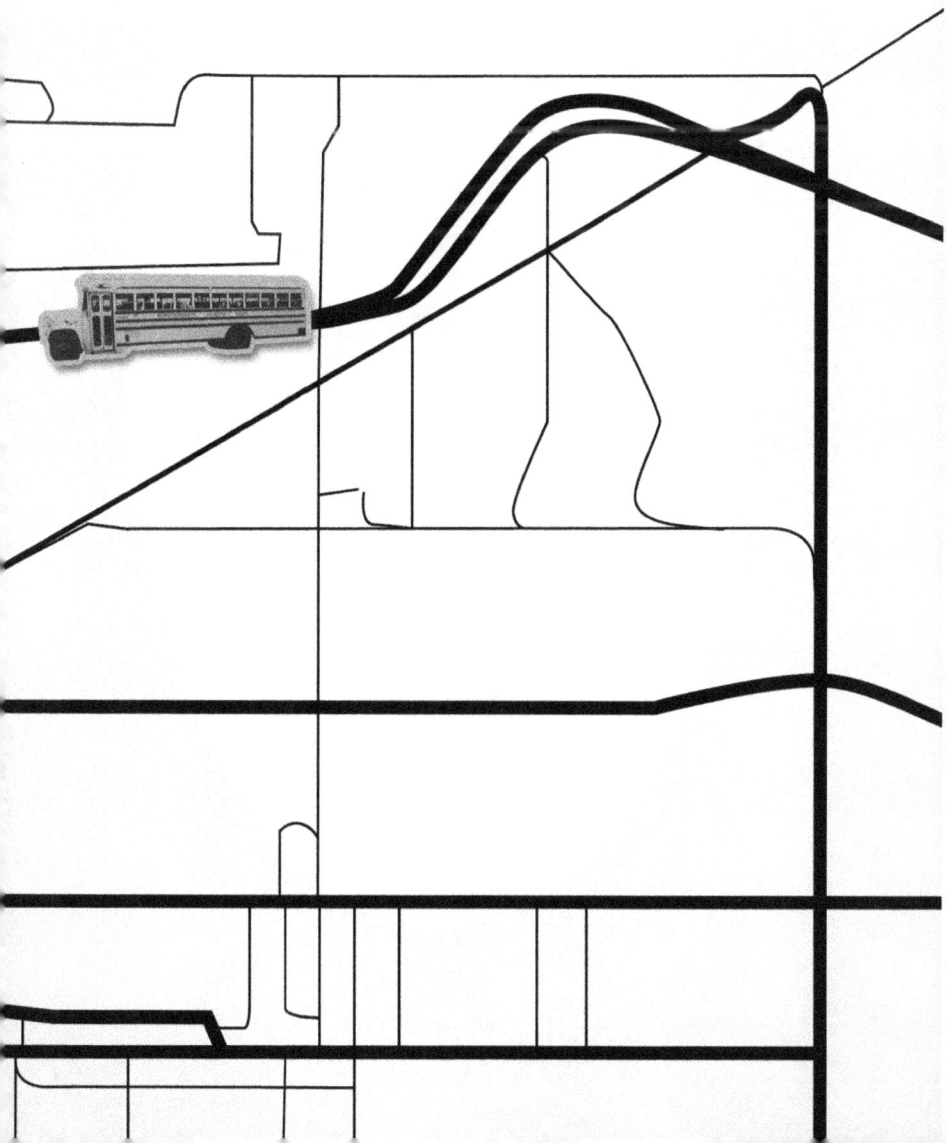

GPS 28: Racism in Education

We've learned that raising and educating your child is like a journey. You have to know where you're starting your trip, where you're going, and the best route to get there. When planning a trip, most people no longer rely on old-fashioned maps because maps don't have updated information about road construction or show the fastest route. Instead, they use GPS systems to help them achieve their goal. In educating and raising children, it would have been nice if the Creator had included an educational GPS or social GPS attached to each child's forehead, but He didn't. You have to find your own GPS system. To help, here are some GPS ideas that can help you overcome common challenges and arrive safely at your destination.

Confronting racism

One serious problem facing parents and children alike is *racism* in the educational system.

Nobody should face racism, especially children. Racism at school or in the educational system exists often in innocuous ways. The corporations often ship black children in lower income neighborhoods to all-white schools in an effort to improve their educational opportunities. However, instead of increasing their educational opportunities, they find themselves isolated with children who are not only of a different race but a different economic background. The school may be too far from home for bussed students to participate in extracurricular activities.

If the child excels in varsity sports, then there is often some sort of adjustment or help given so he or she can participate in the sport. But if he or she simply wants a good education or happens to be interested in the science club rather than the basketball team, he or she will never find parents, coaches or administrators offering to take him or her home from club meetings.

If your child is isolated and sent to a distant school, you have recourse.

First, you must discuss the problems your child faces in his or her new environment. You have to help them acclimate to the situation, but most of all, you must help your child build self-esteem by finding ways he or she can excel in school. Speak to the teachers and remain in close contact. If the child falls behind in any subject, request information on free tutoring services and guide him or her through his or her homework at night.

One way to overcome racism is to be too busy to notice it. The best method of staying busy is study. Instead of children identifying your child as the "black kid who sits behind Jane," the other students will start to identify him or her as "the kid that always knows the answers."

The second thing doesn't involve the child—it's your participation at school board meetings and with the school system itself. Form a neighborhood committee to insist on the abolishment of busing and for the use of those funds for upgrading the local schools. One person can make a difference if he or she fights the establishment with enough conviction.

If the corporation doesn't listen, consider a private school. Often local religious-based schools have tuition scaled to fit family income.

Get involved with the schools and volunteer time. If every concerned parent supported the school with an hour a week, doing any type of task they have the ability to do, from reading stories to helping with maintenance, no matter where the school's location or what type of neighborhood, the school will improve and the level of education will rise.

If your child is in a mixed school and is not a member of the minority but of the majority, teach him or her to respect others regardless of color, creed, economic status, or religion. Racism, religious intolerance and bias based upon economic status begin at home. Even if you don't practice any of these things or speak ill of others, by not discussing the problem and demonstrating your rejection of these practices, you are condoning them.

Discussing racism at home

How do you open the discussion at home? The simplest method used in many classes throughout the United States is the use of a child's eye or hair color. A simple method is to ask a child if blue-eyed people are smarter than those with brown eyes, or if brown-haired people are smarter than those with blond hair. Since many parents have only one child, or if they have several the hair color or eye color is often the same, some parents use the color of articles of clothing to make the point. Since children change the color they wear daily, most children see the folly of basing an impression on appearance or the color of anything, including skin. Laughing at the possibility that the color of your clothing can make you smart transfers easily to racial bias.

Looking ahead

Since there's an African American in the White House, is our society really post-racial?

The racism of the past no longer exists but there are still many pockets of inaccurate beliefs in the school system and society itself. Simply by lowering the norm for passing courses because of economic or racial background, the schools promote racism and the belief that certain races are not capable of achieving the same as others are. If your child's school lowers standards by using such terms as "working to potential," you need to find how the teacher evaluated the child's potential and what the benchmark is for the child's grade level.

"Potential" and "IQ" are both transient. You can raise each through both hard work and greater expectations. Insist on only the best from your child and insist that the teacher do the same. In 1968 this phenomenon was demonstrated in a study by Rosenthal and Jacobson, also called Rosenthal's self-fulfilling prophecy or the Pygmalion Effect. Rosenthal and his partner, Jacobson, gave a test to elementary school children. They told the teacher that the test measured the child's intelligence, and that the results showed that some of the children were gifted while others were slow. The results that the teacher received were actually the locker numbers of the children, yet the teachers expected the children to perform at the level indicated by these random numbers.

Children receive messages both verbally and physically. Make certain the message sent to your child is one of great expectation.

Interracial relationships

Many people still identify with Spencer Tracy in the 1967 movie *Guess Who's Coming to Dinner* and its 2005 remake, *Guess Who,* with Bernie Mac. How do you handle interracial relationships and marriage when you talk to your child?

Love has no boundaries, especially skin color, and children should know this early in life. In school they'll have many friends who are of mixed heritage. When they become teens and adults, children may become involved with someone of different ethnicity. While the color of the skin is not important, the values of the family and cultural belief system may become important in a marriage.

Teaching your child to use logic and giving them a sense of personal integrity and worth is the best way to make certain that no matter whom they select for a life partner, they'll recognize whether that person values them as an individual. It's important to recognize their cultural differences and acknowledge them. Knowing if each is willing to bend in those differences to have a compatible lifelong relationship is important.

Teachers in classrooms with mixed ethnicities

Your child's teacher may be of a different ethnic background or the class is racially mixed. How do you know if the teacher has the training to work in this situation, or is it important?

Talking to the teacher and taking time to work with the school on different projects will give you a good handle on how the teacher handles most situations. Even if you are white and the teacher is also, it's important to understand how they handle the role of race in their classroom. Your teacher is an important role model for your child.

The only way to make certain the teacher has no racial bias to pass to your child is through observation. You can best accomplish this observation through participation in the school and the functions of the school. While most teachers recognize their own unconscious bias through college courses and learn methods of controlling those biases or eliminating them, participation in the schools is another way of also making your school stronger and insuring a better education for your child regardless of the situation.

GPS 29: Bullying

Unfortunately, no trip through childhood and adolescence is ever complete without a stop at "Bully Town, USA." Your child might be a witness to bullying, the recipient of bullying, or even be the bully if you don't take the right road to prevent it early in childhood or have discussions on it at home as soon as you possibly can. Bullying can destroy a child's self-esteem, and as a parent, you don't want it for your own child or anyone's child. Simply plug in "bullying" to your GPS and you'll find how to avoid the roads filled with the bumps and bruises it creates. Even if you end up at Bully Town, the GPS will help you find your way out and back on the road to your destination of a happy and mature adult child.

Give the directions

No child knows what to do without some help. You can use this GPS system to become your child's guide on the road to adulthood.

Bullying is a growing problem. There are all types of bullying including exclusion, rumors, verbal bullying, cyber bullying, and physical bullying. Discussing the issues with your child can help prevent some of them, but not all. Every child feels the pain of exclusion from some groups at one time or another. Sometimes children call names in anger. Each child witnesses someone bullying another person at some point. No matter how you shield your child, bullying occurs.

Rather than shielding and protecting your child, give them weapons to provide their own protection. These weapons start with self-esteem and include knowledge, of not only what to do if he or she is on the receiving end of bullying, but also how to help others if he or she witnesses bullying. Of course, as a parent, you need to emphasize how any type of bullying harms other children and make certain your home isn't a source of bullying. If one parent tends to "lord it over" the house, the child learns to bully at home.

Before you go any further, check your family dynamics. Allowing children to rule the house with bad behavior, and frustration from mixed signals at home are causes of bullying. Parents are the head of the house—there should be no question about that—but providing a clear set of rules, reasons for those rules, and consistent and known punishment will change arbitrary home bullying to good parenting.

Maintaining good communication and love between parents is another key to prevent bullying. No matter how good the GPS system, if the car is malfunctioning, you're not going anywhere.

Developing self-esteem in children helps prevent bullying. Studies show that children with high self-esteem occasionally receive bullying but since it slides off their back like water to oil, it doesn't last long. Self-esteem also gives children confidence to step in if others are bullied. One study shows that only those with high self-confidence helped other children receiving the wrath of a bully. Other studies show that well over half the bullying ceased when observers stepped in and spoke on behalf of the victim. The number of interventions was higher in elementary school; those numbers dropped as age of the child increased. This simply shows the effect of peer pressure and the drop in self-esteem as children enter their teens.

Empathy and bullying

If a child feels the sting of being the outcast, teased, or the object of physical bullying, a parent can help them through the experience with some kind words followed by the phrase, "Now that you know how bad it feels, make sure you never do the same thing to others." Often children become bullies because they've been the objects of bullying along the way. Using an experience as a teaching tool can end the vicious cycle.

A number of children's stories deal with bullying and how the victim over came the problem. Harry Potter was bullied by the Dursleys, by Draco Malfoy, and by others at Hogwarts. When you read to your children, discussing the plight of characters like Harry Potter is one way of opening the door to future discussions.

After hearing of the suicides of several teens because of bullying, Daniel Radcliffe, the star of the *Harry Potter* films, spoke out about children bullied, witnessing bullying and being the bully. One suggestion for all teens that feel desperate was to call the Trevor Lifeline, 1-866-4-U-TREVOR, if they need someone to listen. Discuss the fact with your child on the importance of someone being there for bullied children and make sure you let them know you're there for them too. Take bullying seriously. It doesn't go away by itself unless something in the child's life changes. Can you hear your child say:

Mama, mama can you see
Someone is bullying me

I try to run and hide
I dare not confide

For I am scared
I am totally unprepared

They hunt me in the school hall
God, disappear me into the wall

No one to help me out
Everyone seems to be about

Letting me twist in the wind
I don't have thick skin

I walk alone
I dare not telephone

Anyone for help
Let me hide on the shelf

If I tell someone
Please don't abandon

Me from your care
I cannot look elsewhere

My adolescence is a time
I'm

In conflict about who I am
Like a poor little lamb

That has lost its way
I feel this all day

I look around
I hear the sound

Of kids talking, walking and getting along
I simply don't belong

Doesn't anybody care?
Are they even aware?

That I exist
Have I been dismissed?

My voice yells
With all of my cells

But I cannot hear
I am steeped in fear

The sounds reverberate back within
Am I a person of sin?

I do not count I will not amount
To anything anyhow

Plow me back into the ground
I will no longer be around

— Noise Seventeen from THE LOCKER ROOM
http://mag.inpublicschools.com

Making the best choices

Sometimes children want acceptance from a person or group so badly that they tolerate bullying to receive it. In order to nip this problem before it gets out of hand, the GPS system steers you to self-esteem and selection of friends.

It's not unusual for a child to come to the teacher and tell them that Billy hit him or her, called him or her names or bullied him or her in some other way. If the teacher suggests he or she not play with Billy, the child often says, "But he's my friend." Teaching your child his or her self-importance and how he or she can stand up to a bully are two of the most important lessons you can give. Let your child know that it's okay to end a friendship if the friend is a bully. In fact, it's not just okay—it's the right thing to do. However, there is a way to do it. For this to be effective your child must tell the friend why he or she is ending the relationship. Bullies sometimes don't realize the effect they have on others and will continue until someone intervenes.

Help your child select friends who are supportive by giving the child a guide to friendships. Friends make you feel good about the person you are and help you become better. Help your child make good selections; when a problem occurs, make certain that you listen to their problems and keep an open discussion.

The old-fashioned method

The traditional defense against physical bullying is a martial arts class or self-defense class. Even though this might sound like fighting fire with fire and be somewhat distasteful to some, it works, but for reasons other than often suspected. Most of these classes not only offer techniques in self-protection but also can be real morale boosters with helpful, kind instructors and like-minded students. These build self-esteem and the more self-esteem your child has, the fewer problems he'll have with bullying.

For those who would bully me
I look in the mirror and this is what I see

I am what I am
And this is my telegram

To you who dare
Because you do not care

Or is it your own insecurity
And anatomy

That turns you off
So you get someone else to scoff

And lay your misery on
To you I say be gone

For sticks and stones
Will not break my bones

For sounds are just tones
That postpones

You're looking at yourself
Running around like a little elf

To cause others grief
Turn over a new leaf

For what you did to me
Boomerangs compassionately

For the superior being
Acting

On my behalf
Will get the last laugh

As you hide behind your evil deeds
In the weeds

You will be outed soon
Before high noon

And how stupid you will look
As they throw the book

At everything
Under your wing

That you have done
When you thought that you had won

But business with me
Will not continue to be

As usual
It is unacceptable

And to all who have borne this plight
It is time to get up and fight

To parents who applaud these deeds
Now needs

To teach their children right
And not hide out of sight

For punishment will find its target
And it will be accurate

So look in the mirror with me
Bullies will no longer go scot-free

— Noise Twenty-Eight from THE LOCKER ROOM
http://mag.inpublicschools.com

GPS 30: Behind Closed Doors

Sexuality and that dreaded talk about the birds and the bees with your child are frequently no longer an option unless you begin it in preschool. Even then, the terminology and morality that you prefer go with the talk is wiped away once they learn the hardcore lesson at school or from a friend.

Today we teach our children about sexuality and being "sexy" at far too early an age. Many times, it occurs inadvertently through television shows, the computer or even music. Little Miss pageants take place across the country where parents apply make-up and dress their children in seductive clothing to win a prize. What ever happened to wholesome? What has happened to childhood? In many ways, advertisers, the music industry, television and even the schools have robbed our children of their innocence.

The ideal would be for parents to introduce the topic of sex to their child. However, even in the days before radio, curious children often checked out their plumbing with a member of the opposite sex. Today, the information blatantly assaults the children and the introduction is no longer one of innocence but insistence. You need to look a certain way to attract other people. You need to dance provocatively even at a young age. In schools such as Provincetown, Massachusetts, they even pass out condoms to children in elementary school if they listen to a sex education talk first. Everywhere, people want to "help" the parent with this important lesson to the child.

You need to get a head start on the topic by introducing the facts of life to your child at a young age, even preschool. Rather than sit down and make it a production, most parents simply answer children's questions when they occur. Young children often want to know why Ms. James is so fat. That can be an opportunity to discuss the simple fact of pregnancy and the beginning of a new life. Keeping the discussion simple enough for the child's comprehension, yet answering the question truthfully is the most important part of speaking to them about sexuality.

Everything about the acceptance of sexual preference is now different. At one point, being gay, lesbian or bisexual was a reason parents banned children from their home and held their head down when they walked in public with them. Today, there's much more openness about sexual differences. In fact, some of your children may go to school with a child that has two mommies or two daddies as parents.

The acceptance of alternative lifestyles has made it difficult for parents who don't believe in the morality of the issue. While Christians or those of solid faith in other religions may believe that it's morally wrong, how do they approach it with love and understanding? It is difficult to teach morals in such a way that your child doesn't become hurtful to others faced with issues of sexuality in their family.

Besides approaching the consideration of sexuality in a humane fashion, so it won't affect how your child deals with others, there's another consideration. What if your child finds he or she is more adapted to an alternate sexual lifestyle? If you approach the topic with disdain and disgust, will you in turn make your child hate him or herself and drive a wedge in your relationship with him or her as an adult?

While the issue of choice versus genetic predisposition is still up for grabs, some techniques can help a parent handle this sensitive question, particularly if you're unsure of the answer to the genetics/choice issue. Rather than placing a heavy portion of your talks with your child on the morality of the issue, it might be easier to discuss the difficulties that people face when they chose an alternate sexual lifestyle. You can also emphasize the benefits of a traditional marriage and sexuality. You should also emphasize that every living creature deserves respectful treatment, regardless of his or her sexuality. Those who believe in a loving god can help by reminding children we are all God's creatures.

Even in the strictest of households, sometimes a child announces to their family that he or she is gay. This can be a heart wrenching time for a parent but also a time to get closer to your child than ever before in your relationship. You can use it as a time to turn him or her away from the family or make certain that while you might not approve, you still love him or her and want him or her to know it.

As devastating as the announcement is to the parent, it's also far more difficult for the child in many cases. Keeping the lines of communication open and simply listening at this point is the most any parent can do. Your child often is the most vulnerable and with a strong family support group, he or she can continue to flourish as an adult. Sexuality is only part of the child, not the entire identity, and letting the gay child know that despite this issue, you feel, believe he or she is honorable and beautiful people can allow you to play a future role in his or her life.

Handling matters of sexuality, whether it is a gay/lesbian issue or simply one of dress code, requires a loving caring touch. If not, as a parent, you might face the tragic death of a child by his or her own hands such as that of Tyler Clemente or even worse, the horror of seeing your child drive another to suicide such as the parents of Dharun Ravi and Molly Wie. Either way, the suffering of both should never have occurred.

As far as provocative dress, sexually explicit movies, television, CDs and video games, parents control the wearing apparel and the type of entertainment they allow their child to see. What you believe should reflect in the choices you allow your children. In some cases, there are thoughtful and compelling movies that involve sexuality. Allowing this type of entertainment can actually help if you watch the programs with your child. When you use movies or television programs to start dialogue about the topic of sex with your child, you can open a door to help them understand and allow you to explain your beliefs in a rational manner.

GPS 31: Addictions

The complications of living in our day and age come not only from the permissive society created by earlier generations but also from the rampant use of drugs and acceptance of violence and sexuality. Often school counselors who can't reach parents have to call grandparents to get parents in for conferences. Our society nearly collapses under the additional cost brought on by drugs and other vices. Not only is there increased expense to fight the war on drugs and protect the public from drug users, there's also the cost of caring for addicts, including crack babies and children who suffered mental damage from their mothers' drug or alcohol abuse. Matters become worse when you factor in the use of guns by teens.

No family, no matter how dedicated the parents are, is safe from the pain caused by drug and alcohol abuse. While you can ban the use of drugs in the house, teach your children the hazards of drugs, keep a vigilant eye on the members of your household for signs of drug use and monitor friends and social activities of your children, it deters some problems but does not stop them completely. Children find ways to experiment with drugs or drugs affect families when the families become victims to drug violence. You only have control over one issue, how you deal with the problem in your own house. Successful or unsuccessful, the manner in which you handle either potential makes a difference in the future happiness of your family and cohesiveness of the family unit.

In a perfect world you and all around you would work to keep the children safe from drug and gun use and pressures. However, there is no perfect world and you must make the best of the world in which you exist. In order to prevent drug use by your children, vigilance and awareness are necessary. You must know where the dangers of drugs exist. While Billy, a child's friend, might come from a very good family, the family may be permissive or even use drugs behind closed doors. The family may have a collection of guns that aren't under lock and key. Your own children might seem dedicated to studying at the library but in reality be sitting with the gang out in the woods smoking crack or marijuana or tinkering around with a pistol found at a friend's home. It is your responsibility to find out as much about your children's friends and whereabouts in order to prevent their drug use.

While it might seem imposing to find methods of checking up on your child, it is your responsibility. Until you double check on your child's whereabouts, you won't know whether he or she is telling the truth or not. No matter how you raised your child, children become teens and teens attempt to go against all values their families impose. It is your responsibility to investigate suspicious behavior. There is a dilemma to this vigilance. The dilemma is the question of privacy and trust.

Starting early with an open dialogue with your child is the answer. In most cases, if you let your child know that checking on his or her location is simply part of being a parent and caring, when you do visit the library, it won't be a surprise. Rather than feign a reason to be at the same place he or she is, you need to be direct in your intentions. If you lie, it breeches the trust you hope to develop with your child. Simply tell your child that periodically you'll do this and call it a "reality check."

If you have open dialogue and know your child, then it should be relatively easy to spot behavior that isn't normal for him or her. It is at these times you want to impose vigilance and keep a watchful eye. Call your child and then check his or her location immediately after the call, either through a visit or if you're extremely concerned, a telephone GPS tracker.

Watch for other signs of behavior problems. Loners sometimes become shooters. Parents of children who snap and shoot fellow students at first are surprised. As the weeks wear on, there are numerous reports of signs that the child was in a crisis. However, no one took it to heart enough to check.

Monitoring the friends of your children means knowing the parents. Make it a special point to invite the parents of your child's friends to dinner or visit them. In most cases, you'll find the other parents welcome the visit and want allies in their attempt to raise a good citizen. You don't have to check on the children physically when you know the parents. The comfort level with the parent means you can simply phone to confirm that your child is spending the night there or the mother did take them to the library.

Sometimes, the parents of your child's friends resist meeting with you. It may be something as mundane as time factors or it could be something as treacherous as drug use. It is your responsibility to find out more about the people in either case. Until you know the parents, don't allow your child to spend the night. Tell your child the friend can stay at your house instead.

You cannot simply ignore the facts: drug use is rampant and your child could become one of the statistics. Even if he or she doesn't use, associating with people who do can get him or her into deadly situations. In 2003, The National Drug Intelligence Agency estimated that over seven and a half million children between 12 and 17 used illegal drugs at one time. Studies revealed that 40.2 percent of high school students from grade nine through 12 used marijuana at least once. The same study showed that over 12 percent huffed (used inhalants), 8.7 percent tried cocaine, over 11 percent tried ecstasy, 6.1 percent used illegal steroids, almost 9 percent tried cocaine, 3.3 percent tried heroin and finally over three percent injected an illegal substance at least once.

You cannot trust the children to be safe at school since the study showed that nationwide, almost thirty percent of the children received illegal drugs or had an opportunity to purchase illegal drugs at school in the year before they took the survey. One final fact that should scare every parent is that of all those surveyed, almost six percent of the children used marijuana on school property within thirty days preceding the survey.

Children often don't have to go beyond their medicine chest or storage area to find drugs for their use. Look at your home environment to see if you're supplying your child with materials for huffing. Do you have prescription drugs in your medicine chest? Teens even consume heart medication, antibiotics or other pills in an attempt to find a drug high. Often this consumption has dire results. Discuss any medication you have in the house on a regular basis to let your child know they can't get high from it but can get sick. If you use psychotropic drugs for depression or anxiety, keep them under lock and key. Eliminate alcohol and guns from your home or keep them locked in a cabinet.

You cannot control the outside environment but you can control your own home, your behavior and the access your child has to drugs or guns. Open dialogue at your home gives you a chance to watch for any warning signs. If you know your child and keep an eye open for odd behavior, you'll often divert a problem before it starts. Even keeping a close watch won't stop your child if there's peer pressure, but it can alert you to a problem so you can handle it early.

GPS 32: Homeschooling

An increasing number of parents are investigating the potential of homeschooling as an alternative to entering public schools. Just like public school situations, when you teach your child at home there are many roadblocks and dangers along the way. In order to avoid these, the GPS system can help guide you on the appropriate path that helps you decide whether homeschooling is the right choice for your situation.

Why choose homeschooling?

A survey conducted by the National Center for Educational Statistics in 2003 questioned over a million households that homeschooled their children and found most families had several reasons for doing it. The biggest majority, almost 49%, felt they could give their child a better education in the home. A little over 38% had religious reasons, with 27% of the parents citing the public schools as a poor learning environment. Some of the families simply said homeschooling was for family reasons and gave no more information.

Fifteen percent of the homeschooling parents wanted to develop their child's moral character and didn't feel the public school environment could do this. About 12% felt that the schools taught concepts contrary to their beliefs and another 12% did not feel the schools offered challenging enough material or lessons.

Between 8% and 9% of the responses came from parents with students who had behavior problems and children who had special needs.

Your reason for homeschooling probably falls into one of the above groups. If you feel the schools are failing, you have to ask yourself not only how are they failing but also why you feel you can do better. Are you being arrogant or simply honest?

Even the word "homeschooling" has evolved to meet its growing place in society. The homeschooling revolution has taken on a life of its own with the numbers increasing from 345,000 in 1994 to an estimated number of over two million in 2010. With the increased popularity, it is no longer a two-word descriptor but has become a single word, homeschooling, to describe parents who take the responsibility for their child's education. The process is often unlike the traditional schools so it isn't simply school taking place in the home, but uses the Internet, tutorial programs, community service, field trips, and alternative learning experiences for the child's education. Because of this, changing the word to one new one is the path that most describes the process.

An arrogant parent doesn't feel he or she needs additional materials or help with schooling his or her child. He or she simply believes he or she has all the answers and needs no other advice on teaching or additional help from programmed instruction. Conversely, a parent who feels the need to homeschool because of failures in the school system or the inability to get special help for their child often spends hours researching the process of homeschooling before making the leap into it.

Socialization and homeschooling

One of the biggest concerns most parents have before embarking on the road to homeschooling is the socialization of their child. Without the traditional school activities and the interaction with other children, is it possible to raise a well-rounded individual?

The answer comes from the GPS system that guides you to

extracurricular activities such as church youth groups, music and art lessons, Little League, the YMCA programs, Scouts, academic contests like spelling bees, field trips, 4-H Clubs, and affiliation with other homeschooled children and neighborhood children.

Local homeschool support groups often have activities for families and homeschooled children. These might be special classes offered to the group such as physical education classes or periodic field trips sponsored by the group. State associations for homeschooled children offer contests such as science fairs and spelling bees. Local groups may have bowling teams, bands or choirs in addition to co-sponsored yearbooks and graduation ceremonies.

Societal outcast?

Many studies show that children who are homeschooled not only socialize well with others their own age but also with those of other age groups and adults. One such study was conducted by John Wesley Taylor. Using the Piers-Harris Children's Self-Concept Scale, he evaluated 224 homeschooled children. The study found that more than 50% of homeschooled children ranked in the 90th percentile for healthy self-esteem. Of the group tested, only 10% ranked below the national average. This is a good indicator of the child's ability to function in society.

Rather than being rejected by society, most studies show the children function far better in society than most public schooled or private schooled children. Since they have the freedom to explore more areas and interact with more than simply their peers, home-schooled children find the transition to the world of grown-ups far easier. They often don't face the need to please their peers like the private and public school child does.

Should you homeschool?

Making the decision to homeschool isn't an easy one and you shouldn't take it lightly. It requires hours of dedication both in establishing the curriculum and the process of teaching. There is no break from the children and you'll need to make certain that you carve out time for yourself. Taking personal time is not a way of avoiding your responsibility to your child, but it's a way of ensuring you're providing the best educational environment possible.

If your resources are limited, support groups are often the answer. Many of the support groups offer a way to make time. Sometimes parents bond and form combined courses. By doing this, one parent handles both groups of students and allows the other a quick day of reprieve and rest. Other parents simply take a day away that's marked as a school holiday, send the child to a parent's or leave them with another caretaker to get a rest from parenting and teaching. Some parents use the time when children are in extracurricular activities, such as story time, for their alone time.

There are a variety of curriculum programs available to aid parents in homeschooling. Many of the homeschooling support groups also are a valuable source to access the best materials or programs. Some online programs or distance learning programs can also be beneficial for the parent who decides to homeschool.

It is necessary to keep records of the subjects, hours spent, and accomplishments of the child. In order to enter college, your child needs a transcript. Schools provide this easily through simply recording the class and the grade. You'll need to keep your own transcript if you later enter your child in any other type of formal education. Most states and colleges offer a list of requirements necessary to consider your child a high school graduate. You have to provide the records that prove your child accomplished it.

What makes a great teacher?

No matter whether it's in a public school or homeschool, a great teacher is someone who *cares*. Parents of course, should fit this description. Most statistics show that homeschooled children far excel at standardized tests over their public school counterparts, regardless of the parent's academic or financial background. The key is the parent's love. Taking homeschooling seriously and maintaining your insistence on the completion of work is only part of the process. Loving your children and letting them know they are loved is the key to success in any schooling, including homeschooling.

GPS 33: The "Good Old Days"

In an ever-changing world, it's often difficult to understand what is important and valuable from the past and what is no longer necessary. A perfect example of this is the length of the school year. In earlier days, the children needed to help parents in the field so the school year coincided with the planting and harvesting of crops. Today very few people work on farms, let alone have their child help in the fields. Yet, we still maintain the same school year.

We changed from a society that believed the teachers were demi-gods with mystical abilities and the only experts on children. With those beliefs came the adherence to punishment of our children for any infraction at school. Instead some arrived at a belief that the school system and teachers know nothing and instead of following through for reprimands at school, they sue the system for damage to our child's psyche. Others simply gave up all responsibility and involvement in the education of their child.

We have gone from a single language to bilingual and English as a second language. At one time, the sponsors for immigrants were the interpreters. Today the government and their entities such as the schools are responsible for that task. Unfortunately, because of this, the budgets of governmental agencies, already overloaded, now bear an additional burden. The question now arises, should the schools be responsible for classes in English as a second language? In some countries such as Canada, there are two languages, both English and French. Should this be a consideration? Capacity to speak more then one language is valuable in a world of many countries and races.

Our schools have changed from simple institutions where children learn both literally and figuratively through sex education and other classes that strip any moral value or belief from the subject matter. The theory of evolution was a scandal when Darwin first suggested it. Then the trend changed where it was scandalous to mention the potential of a divine creation. Today intelligent design and evolution both hold a place in the classroom.

We feed our children's minds with the rudiments of reading and math early in their lives and yet our drop out rate climbs and test scores continue to drop. Rather than focusing on the fact this plan doesn't seem to work, we hit it even harder with more funds and attention. Only today is our society looking at systems that work and finding out why they do.

Our society is no longer as simple as it was. In the second largest hospital in the United States, Parkland Memorial Hospital in Dallas, 70 percent of the births were to illegal residents with many having a second child. The lack of a true immigration program creates confusion for the schools and the population. Should we simply ignore the group or do something about them? If you take action, what should it be? Should laws change giving amnesty, should the borders be open or should we simply follow the law as it stands and deport all unregistered aliens? Until there's an answer, this group of the population will remain in the background, never participating in the education of their children for fear of discovery.

The answers are not simple nor can they be status quo. Status quo hasn't worked for a long time and it reflects in the academic scores and drop out rates. While some things have changed, there is question to whether they've changed for the better. As a nation, we are no longer responsible for our own actions. We have become a litigious society that sues others for our own mistakes. One woman sued a store because an unruly child made her fall. She won even though that young child was her own. This is one of many incidences where the courts ruled that parents are no longer responsible for their charges or themselves.

We need a framework that allows for input. The framework needs to include self-responsibility, parental input and yet allow for the diverse nation we've become. Our schools have become neutral on morality in fear of lawsuits. There seems to be no right or wrong. Because of the dilemma of pleasing everyone and offending no one, there is only chaos in the schools. It is much like the patients running the mental institution. We have not trained the children in proper behavior and yet we give them full reign over their lives in the classroom.

Today, the suggestion of any religious ideology brings on the full forces of the ACLU. How can we train a child in right and wrong when parents give up the obligation to the school system and the schools have no power to do it?

America can turn around the schools but it will take more work, a change of attitude and cooperation of the schools, parents and community. There is a place for moral lessons in the schools but that should start at home and be the responsibility of the parents. However, self-responsibility is a moral value that schools, parents and community should teach and enforce. Starting there, we can make greater strides with the students understanding their role in the educational process.

Programs promoting community involvement in the schools can produce an attitude that gives education and the privilege of an education the honor it deserves. At one time the schools and the church were the center of all functions for the community. Bringing back the focus on the schools can elevate the importance of education and make a huge difference in attitude.

Bringing in help and input from the community through an increased awareness can help relieve the frustration of taxpayers, knowing they have a say in the process. It also can lower the tax burden and improve the quality of education. Programs directed at parents to teach them how to help their children and open the door for more input in the schools are positive ideas that have long fallen to the wayside with the one room schoolhouse.

No one suggests we go back to the day when a switch was the answer for an unruly child or a ruler to the knuckles solved the problem of a child not paying attention. However, there are many ideas from the past that would work today if implemented. Involvement, self-responsibility and a higher regard for the educational process could make a huge difference in our declining educational system.

GPS 34: Technology 101

The problems you faced as a child or teenager still exist. However, with today's technology and fast moving pace, the effects on the child accelerate at a pace faster than most of us understand. Not only do they accelerate, the technological changes also complicate many of the issues parents faced as teens.

Cyber bullying, pornographic websites, text messaging and chat room predators were never part of most parents' lives when they were young. Today it's common to find children investigating sexuality on the Internet or meeting people far older than themselves in chat rooms. If you aren't familiar with the computer, you need to become familiar or you won't know what's going on in your house.

Simply learning the language of the text message can be helpful to any parent who wants to maintain his or her status as head of the household. Acronyms for complete sentences now hold meaning for many of the young but parents remain clueless. Messages may contain vital information you should know to keep your child from harm or life-altering mischief. Simply learning the language of the text message can help you become more adept at knowing what your child is doing.

There's never been a substitute for knowing your child's friends. Encourage your child to invite friends over to your home so you can judge their personality and propensity toward trouble with first hand knowledge. You can observe them in relaxed behavior and see if the computer is the sole source of entertainment. If it is, you need to learn to read the computer history, learn to block certain websites from your child and most of all, have open dialogue with him or her about chat rooms, social networking websites and giving out email addresses to strangers.

Even though the technology is different, the importance of keeping an open dialogue with your child hasn't changed. Setting rules and regulations for the use of cell phones is another important part of parenting today. Too many parents give their children cells phones with unlimited texting and phone minutes. The problem is, where are they spending those minutes? Too frequently, the ability to text unlimited messages allows the child to exist in a cyber world you can't enter.

If your child is like most, he or she already has a cell phone. Most parents purchase them so they can contact the child to check location or the child can contact them to check in or in cases of emergency. However, unrestricted access allows him or her to do crazy things such as send nude photos, cyber bully or contact strangers he or she met in a chat room. A cell phone call never really tells you where your child is, it simply tells you where your child wants you to think he is.

There is new technology available for parents that come imbedded in cell phones. It transmits the location of the person holding the cell phone and you can simply log into a site to find the child's location as long as he or she is carrying the phone. You can also find the historic location information for as far back as thirty days. If your child drives, the speed and direction of the phone is also available.

While this type of technology seems like an imposition on the child's privacy rights, as a parent, your responsibility to protect the child is more important. Giving a young child a phone like this can help you find your son or daughter in the event someone attempts to steal him or her away from you. With older children, the usefulness is obvious. You can find out if they're driving at excessive speeds, going places you don't want them to go or allow you to check without calling and making yourself "the worrywart."

Some parents use these types of devices to a limited degree.

They might check to see where the child is if the home arrival isn't at the time requested or never use the program at all, but simply know it's there in case of emergency. Other parents may use it immediately and either begin a program to correct misbehavior or set their minds at ease that their child follows the rules of the house. If you use one of these phones, make certain that you erase the history after you go to the website if you don't tell your children about the phone GPS.

Of course, this brings us to another dilemma. Are you teaching your child to become less than truthful by your example? That is something you'll have to decide on your own. The morality of being a concerned parent or being 100 percent honest weighs heavily with good points for both sides. As the head of your house, you must make that decision for yourself. There are many factors involved, some of which include the child's personality, his or her age and your personal philosophy.

Computer games and gaming websites also have a great deal of influence on your child. Most parents find that monitoring the type of games their child plays is important. Your personal belief in whether your child will learn violent tendencies from playing action packed war games varies in each person's house. Other things in the computer games may be a red flag to parents.

Nudity and sexuality are part of many games. Read the gaming package and experience the game with your child the first time he or she plays. You'll learn a lot about the game and find anything objectionable with this action. In addition to that, you'll also be spending time with your child in an activity he or she enjoys.

With every new piece of technology comes a new danger to the family or your child. Make certain that you limit time on the phone or other electronic devices to make family time. Family time can include a time for physical activity or simply time to talk to one another, something families today seldom do. Remember that you need to monitor your own time on the computer too. Too frequently, parents find themselves engrossed in Facebook or other social networks and block the family while they are. Be a good example for your child and limit your personal time too.

GPS 35: How to Use the Political System

It doesn't surprise anyone to find that the promises made by political candidates are often empty and disappear once the official is elected. However, that doesn't have to be the case if you effectively set your GPS to make the officials accountable. The process is a long one and requires that you follow the directions as far as you can take them and even acquire a few fellow travelers to join you on the road to improving the school systems.

Finding officials who work toward change

Every November, a ray of new hope comes from the elections. But many voters become disillusioned because they haven't taken the time to listen to the issues or rationalize how the candidates hope to accomplish their promises. In other words, the candidates' speeches and commercials are written to give the most pleasing verbiage to the masses. When campaigning, a county auditor might say he or she will save the Social Security system, knowing most people have no idea that the auditor has nothing to do with it and the voters won't bother to ask. Congressional candidates might tell you they have improvements in mind to save the educational system, but never specify the actual improvements or the implementation of them. They simply tell you that they support education. But then, doesn't every American want a better educational system and support the efforts to create it?

Set your GPS to find a group of like-minded people to help

you find the best candidates for educational reform. They don't have to be national candidates, although some can be, but can be local board members with innovative ideas and logic. Listen to all the political rhetoric and consider the positions held by the candidates, and then prepare to attend live sessions where candidates answer questions from the audience. Having several people in your group helps accomplish your task. Since you have more people, the probability of being called on to ask a question increases.

Prepare a list of questions for each promise. If a candidate intends to cut the budget while increasing the efficiency of the school, ask how. If he or she wants to supply the schools with innovative programs, ask what the programs are, how he or she will find them, and the method of infusing the schools with the program. If there is no answer, your next question is then, "How can we believe your promise when you have no plan or knowledge of the subject?"

Making friends and making contacts

Your local parent organization for the school is a good place to begin your process to find like-minded individuals. If you have a candidate whom you particularly like and don't want to confront him or her with issues in public but you do want to give him or her a chance to prepare a plan of action, join his or her campaign. Sincere candidates appreciate people who want to know how they intend to accomplish the mission they set for themselves in campaign promises. They also appreciate the heads-up on important questions someone else could surprise them with on the campaign trail. You'll make friends and connections that can be valuable later.

Find candidates who don't believe that big government has all the answers or that simply throwing money at the school system fixes everything. Years of money tossing have not produced improved schools. In fact, our schools are in worse shape than they were before many of the high-dollar programs began. Look for candidates who offer alternatives and potential for more parental involvement in the educational decision making process. Consider candidates who want to protect the schools from frivolous suits that create anxiety, destroy educational quality, and can cost millions of dollars.

Consider candidates who believe that improving local schools is far better than busing children to other schools. Someone still goes to the local schools; busing just takes away from the funds to improve them. Candidates who think logically often negate the practice. In fact, people who understand education, and not just finance, often make the best choices.

The votes are counted

Once the election is over and a candidate has won, make him or her accountable. Any group formed during the campaign should ride forward together with the GPS system aimed at educational improvement. Stay current and stay in the political scene. It's too easy to turn your back and think everything will be okay now that Mr. X is in office. The truth is that unless you continue to ask hard questions and be involved, it won't be okay.

Take every opportunity to attend board meetings. Make your presence known, particularly if you disagree with the direction the board takes. When you agree, show your support and let the board members know. Too often people criticize without ever praising. Just like any other person, members of the school board deserve support when you feel they're on the mark. You'll build esteem in their eyes for your fairness, and when you bring an issue to the board they'll be more likely to listen.

Congressional candidates and state candidates tend to

promise many things without producing results. Keep letter-writing campaigns going in your area, reminding the candidate of his or her promises. The more letters they receive, the more they're aware of voter dissention and that there's always another election coming.

Almost all politicians have a public phone number for questions, suggestions and complaints. Use them and keep your grassroots group aware of the number so they can call too. Sometimes, you'll find that the promises made can't be kept because of red tape or lack of support from other members of Congress or other offices. In this case, work on the source of the problem with the same tenacity that you use on your local politician. Contact groups in other areas for more support.

Not all politicians are bad

The political arena is filled with compromise and promises. In many cases, in order to get a bill passed, funding for "pork-barrel" projects in specific states or districts is included. If you have an honest politician who truly wants the best for the country, he or she recognizes that sometimes the tradeoff is too great. If your candidate has that problem, he or she will let you know. He or she can tell you exactly why he or she voted for a specific bill or didn't vote. While he or she may not have given you what you wanted, he or she may have saved thousands of taxpayer's dollars or prevented a law included in the bill that could harm the country. No GPS system works if there's bad communication. Keep an open mind and an open line of communication and your GPS system will guide you in the right direction.

GPS 36: Working Through Intimidation – On Both Sides

In any situation, one person can make a difference if that one person has conviction. Changing the system isn't easy and it isn't for the faint of heart, especially when it comes to education. Teachers and administrators, after all, have years of training, so they firmly believe what they're doing is right. The school board members have the backing of the electorate or a high-ranking official appoints them, so they believe they're right. If you find there is a flaw in the system, you must have the same conviction to follow through with your belief.

Maybe you don't wish to shake the tree for fear that it could come crashing down on your child's academic career. It is a concern. However, the approach you take can make all the difference in the world. Rather than flaring up in anger and engaging in finger pointing, the best methods of dissention are your persuasive powers and charm.

Communication experts say that if you say two positive things followed by your negative and then another positive, people will listen. Everyone wants to hear the positive and because of that, people will listen to your complaint and really hear it, rather than simply pretend to listen and give a stock response. Even if you aren't a fan of the school board or the teacher, you can find something positive to say. Here is an example of a parent attempting to persuade the board and teachers to set higher standards for the classroom.

"I'm a parent of a student in grade six, and I'm delighted that my child attends this school and is in Mrs. Jones's homeroom. Mrs. Jones is a very caring teacher and the school board members are fair and just men and women. I fear, however, despite their good intentions, they're overlooking a problem.

"Our children are being shortchanged. While the members of the board and the teacher may feel they're giving our boys and girls an opportunity to succeed by lowering achievement standards, in reality it is a life sentence to failure. By expecting less from them, we are telling our children they are not capable and we are turning out inadequately trained students. I realize the board and Mrs. Jones only want the best for the children but I don't understand how lowering standards helps them succeed. What can we do to reverse this trend and how can parents help so that we no longer expect less than the best from our children?"

This short speech praises the board and teachers but doesn't point fingers at anyone. It's a "looking for solutions" comment that also drives home the point that the system is inadequate. The speech ends with a question that begs for an answer.

In most cases, someone will attempt to either answer the question or fluff you off with gibberish, hoping you'll nod and sit down without any response. Listen carefully. If you don't understand, feel comfortable saying, "Could you please explain that in terms that I can understand? I am not following you."

School boards and teachers faced with difficult questions they can't answer often don't expect people to voice their frailties. They hope that by talking over your head, you'll feel inadequate and go away. By saying you don't understand, you'll force them to speak in common terms and be able to see through the veil of pseudo-educational garble.

If at that point they fluff you off, you have a right to become more insistent. They hold your child's future in their hands. You've conducted yourself with dignity and others listening can see that. Everyone roots for the underdog. If the board or teacher puts you down, it makes you the underdog and you'll immediately have the backing of the people in the audience. While no one wants to be humiliated, admitting frailties first can prevent that. No one can make you feel small or inadequate unless you accept his or her opinion. As a parent, your child deserves your backing for the best possible education. To save your child you would probably throw yourself in the path of a moving car; embarrassment is a small price to pay by comparison.

Perhaps the problem isn't one of a broad nature but one of family reputation. Maybe your older children, for some reason, were troublemakers, but your younger children are not, even though the teachers attribute that reputation to them. You need to visit each teacher at the beginning of the year and make it clear that the younger children do not have the same problems of other children in the family. You aren't being disloyal to the children who had poor grades or were troublemakers; you're just being honest with the teacher. By discussing the problem before the first grade cards, you'll make the teacher look at the behavior or accomplishments with a fresh eye before they form an opinion.

Even the most eloquent of speakers sometimes can't divert a bully, and school boards or teachers can be bullies too. If you find that the board or teachers bury your concerns under the table (to protect the school system from exposure and ultimately lawsuits, or simply because those in power feel the need to always be right), take it to the public. Start a campaign to expose the situation. One person *can* make a difference. I will repeat that one person can make a difference because it's something you'll need to repeat to yourself frequently.

Write letters to the editor or contact local news stations and newspapers. Contact other parents to get support. Write to the Departments of Education, both state and national, exposing the problem. Write your congressional representatives, both state and federal. Write the mayor. Write to the governor of your state. Write anyone and everyone who has anything to do with the schools. It isn't a huge task and only requires one compelling letter adjusted slightly for each person or organization.

Never forget the phrase, "Right makes might." If you firmly believe you're right, then go down for the count and do whatever it takes to change the system. In the process, you become the teacher. You teach your child and those around you never to give up when you know you're right and the battle is important. With your example you'll not only earn the respect of your child, you'll make your child a stronger and more determined adult.

GPS 37: Empower Education Empower

I encourage you to visit www.empower-education-empower. com. Starting with its index and throughout each page, this website presents opportunities for conversation.

Up front it asks the reader questions that can be discussed in the website's town hall chat rooms. Here's a sample:

— Are the classrooms today providing everything that students need?

— Do teachers receive the same backing and support of yesteryear?

— Are parents happy with the role the school plays in their children's lives?

— Do members of the community feel the money they send to the schools benefits their businesses or life?

These are tough questions that have no right answer. The role of this website is to look for ways to improve the schools and to help lower the cost of education while improving the quality.

Schools today have become big business with little room for the input from the average parent, teacher, or student, let alone the taxpayer footing the bill. But one person can make a difference. That's the concept of the website. Through dialogue backed by action, you can return the schools to the center of learning and social function for the community.

But it isn't easy.

Each person needs to speak his or her mind on issues that affect everyone. No matter what your age, the role of the school and quality of education has an impact on your life. Older people with no children in the house feel the sting of increasing property taxes. Parents watch as their child loses hours of education because of bad behavior of others in the classroom. Teachers face the problem with their hands tied and administrations expect them to perform miracles in the classroom while offering no support. Students who want to learn are ridiculed for wanting a better education, as bullies take over the class and take retribution on those who are more dedicated.

The next generation of students will become the leaders and workers of the world. If the workers cannot adequately read, do the simplest of math, understand basic concepts or follow directions, what will happen to the state of our country? Already America is falling behind other nations in the quality of learning. We set our standards lower and lower every year and the students fulfill our constantly decreasingly expectations. It's time to rise up and regain the respect for education, improve the classroom, and do what past teachers, parents, communities and students failed to do. We need change back to original virtues, beliefs and standards that somehow went to the wayside. The past has shown that education without discipline; demands without consequences, and belief without action don't work.

Educating our students is a task for every member of the community whether they have children in school, are students or teachers, or are simply active members of society. By joining forces and viewing education through each other's eyes, together we can find the answers.

The dedication of this website to the people of the American communities who still believe that education is the answer begins with talking points. The points made in these articles aren't always the right answers but they are places to begin discourse. If you believe that change is necessary, then join in and together we'll find an answer.

As part of the examination of the issues, the website looks at five important players in the process:

1. Parents

2. Teachers

3. Students

4. Communities

5. Government

In looking at these players, discussions around these categories are available:

– Traditions

– Choice

– Discipline

– Economics

– Support

– Effectiveness

Here are samples of what effective parents, teachers, students, communities and government look like:

Parents

Everyone is in such a hurry to sign their children up for athletic teams and after school activities that family mealtime is almost non-existent. Meals used to be the best time to discuss the occurrences of the day, impart knowledge, and give the child the benefit of your beliefs and experiences. Today, because of busy schedules, the strong family unit isn't as common. If you really want to make the effort, you can change that.

Assign one night a week as a family night. You can have the

night rotate according to the family's commitments but never omit the opportunity for a meal together followed by games or a movie. Family night can take place in your own home or be an evening of bowling or other sport where everyone participates. You can take walks, bicycle, or even play a rousing board game together. The idea of family night is not about what you do, but focuses on being together.

Select the movies carefully that you show in your home. Make certain they impart your beliefs and ideals. Discussing a movie can expose your child to your belief system in a low-key, palatable manner.

Teach your child the rules of the house and stick to those rules. Children function in society best when they possess the quality of self-discipline. They either learn this at home or receive far more difficult learning sessions when they attend school. Consistent and easily identified rules, and clear consequences if they're broken, help you mold your child into a good citizen in both school and community.

Have a good discussion of events that involve moral dilemmas. Be honest with your opinions and see what your child would do or how he or she feels on the topic. Sometimes noting that a person was caught doing something wrong or lying to avoid punishment can trigger a good discussion that helps your child understand how they let people down when they don't follow moral guidelines for his or her behavior.

Remember that sometimes discipline simply means that you let your child know your disappointment. You don't have to threaten a child with bodily harm, scream, or send him or her to his or her room until he or she reaches voting age; you simply have to address problems. Sometimes a quiet voice of reason works more wonders than a stiff punishment. Know when each is the appropriate action.

Respect your child and show him or her the type of respect

you expect in return. If you treat a child in a respectful manner, he or she learns to do the same for others. Unfortunately, that doesn't mean that he or she always shows *you* respect. When children disrespect you, there should be repercussions for the behavior.

While children learn where they live, they also live outside the confines of the family—in school, at friends' houses, and in the neighborhood. If they bring home behavior that doesn't fit your belief system, you need to sternly remind them and then correct the behavior with appropriate punishment.

Love your children and help them become lovable. Society does not love whining, rude monsters. You owe it to your children to help them be welcomed members of the community. Talk to them, read to them and impart to them a love of learning. Spend time together, respect them, discipline bad behavior, encourage and praise the good, and most of all, let them know you love them no matter what. Be a part of your children's lives to insure that they become valuable community members and good students.

Teachers

Every good teacher understands that children learn different ways, possess different levels of comprehension for a particular subject, enjoy some subjects more than others, and have different levels of attention spans. Because of this, the traditional method of teaching all children with one style, or even in-group learning, is not inclusive enough to provide the necessary training for a range of individual children.

In order to achieve the most success in the classroom each teacher should dedicate classroom time to tackling the job of finding the key that unlocks the potential for each child. When a lesson is child-specific, then true learning can take place for all.

This is not an easy task, however. It requires knowing each child well and making the learning inclusive to best utilize his or her strengths and strengthen his or her weaknesses. While the initial tests each year can show comprehension levels, they don't present any information on the preferences of a child for a topic or particular style of learning. Observation tends to be the best method of finding this information.

Teachers have a busy day and it can be difficult to create individual lesson plans, particularly in today's crowded classrooms. However, there are ways to make the time for this important mission. Materials presented in a modular fashion can help. The modules base the material on different reading levels, levels of comprehension, strengths and weaknesses in learning. Each child participates by selecting a lesson from the module based on the assessment of the teacher, studying it, and self-testing.

Unlocking the capabilities of the child requires that the teacher also consider the type of learning that best suits the child. This includes the child's ability to learn through tactile/kinesthetic, visual, or auditory pathways, and providing appropriate materials for each style. Learning areas with tape recorders, raised letters, visual materials and lessons that involve activity are perfect to help each child use his or her special learning style.

Sometimes simply having a safe atmosphere in which to learn is the most important thing a timid learner needs to excel. A safe learning environment can simply mean providing encouraging words for the child who has concluded that he or she is a failure and doomed to that position for the rest of his or her life. Without the belief that achievement is possible, no child will ever reach beyond his present level of accomplishment and journey to the next plateau. Not only is positive reinforcement important but also lessons designed to utilize the style and strengths of the child so it's inclusive of his or her abilities and belief.

When the teacher makes the classroom a positive learning environment for each child and works on his or her interaction skills, reading skills and other basics, the child's grades and scores for standardized tests increase also. The learning centers geared to learning style can accommodate almost all children in the classroom. Learning modules geared to specific accomplishment levels are available to use repeatedly, so once created, they don't require extra time. Providing a nurturing learning environment takes no extra time and costs nothing. These steps help each child develop at his or her own pace in his or her own way. You don't have to teach to the test to see great results. You simply have to teach to the child.

Students

Are your schools effective in delivering a good education? Parents ask this question all the time but it's important for students to do the same. Sometimes, students have no idea what they should look for in the classroom. They've never experienced anything different and because of this they believe what they experience is the best they can expect from school.

Some basic facts should help you decide whether or not your school is effective. If you can answer "yes" to the questions below, you're one of the lucky students who has the opportunity to attend an effective school.

1. Do you spend more time on lessons than on waiting for the teacher to get the class under control?

A "yes" to this question means that your school considers orderly conduct important, and students have the opportunity to decide whether they want to learn or simply quietly attend the class. The teacher can't force a student to learn but he or she can create an environment that's conducive to learning. This type of environment is one where the teacher has a firm control over the activities of the class.

2. Do you look forward to going to school because there's always something interesting to do?

Activities make learning fun. If your teacher finds ways to get you involved in the process of learning, you'll probably learn more and take an active interest in the subject matter. This is far better than sitting quietly listening to a lecture, although, sometimes lectures on topics can be exciting too.

3. Do you spend most of your school day in the classroom?

Many students have to ride buses to school. If they live in a rural area, a long ride to the nearest school is to be expected. However, if they have a long bus ride and there are schools far closer than the one they attend, then they are wasting time. Schools that utilize the student's time as advantageously as they utilize financial resources are far more effective than those that don't.

4. Does your school reward hard work and good behavior and offer fast and consistent punishment for bad behavior?

Schools that reward those who perform in classes the way they are expected tend to have better students and be more effective than schools that take a lax attitude. Some schools are soft on bad behavior and offer multiple chances to those that breech the rules, or fail to offer any type of meaningful punishment. This only encourages poor behavior and reduces the effectiveness of the school. The more rapid the punishment, the more effective it is.

5. Does your school encourage a sense of pride in yourself, your school, and your community?

An effective school does all three. It helps students become the best they can be and promotes school and community activity. This type of school builds good citizens for not just the school but also the world.

Communities

Every child needs an opportunity to demonstrate what he or she has to offer the world outside the classroom. While most people feel that learning takes place only in the school, nothing could be further from the truth. Children and adolescents learn through experiences in school but also in the "real world." The community can make that learning positive by providing a nurturing environment filled with learning opportunities.

If you don't have a child of school age, it doesn't mean that you aren't a potential role model for someone else's child. Today there are broken homes across the land. Often families have only one parent to handle the rigors of raising a child. While you might not feel you or your community can make a difference in a child's life, think again.

Your community can organize opportunities for learning experiences and reap an abundance of rewards at the same time. These opportunities don't require money but they often require time and dedication to young people. Simple examples include the Big Brother, Big Sister programs that give children the benefit of adults in their life. These are well-known opportunities but there are others, which communities can adopt to increase the learning levels of children in their districts.

Besides bringing a sense of personal satisfaction to those who volunteer, working with children in the community can actually save money. When test scores are higher and children test high on scores, you don't have to pour money into the school system. More money doesn't necessarily create more learning, but unfortunately many communities believe that money is the only answer. You need to show children the value of education and make learning part of the community.

If you own a business, hire a school-age child to perform some of the tasks that don't require expertise in a specific field. Children learn by observation. If there's an opportunity for them to have hands-on instruction in a specific skill, take a minute to show them how to do the task. If you have books that help the child further his or her knowledge in your field, provide him or her with the reading material. Create a nurturing but professional environment and be not only a good boss but also an adult who cares about the child. Ask about school, grades, and other things to show that you care. Encourage education.

The money that your youthful employee receives also provides a good lesson in math and economics. It will boost the child's self-esteem, something that often ensures better grades and behavior in the school.

Get active with the school system. If you have a farm, business, or manufacturing plant, invite the school to have field trips. Volunteer to tutor in the schools. Provide material for crafts and classroom projects. Often people and businesses throw away many items that schools could use for various projects. Take one afternoon a year to visit the school and tell about the work you do.

Some communities work with schools on programs that benefit everyone. They find empty overgrown lots, till the soil, then divide the lots into sections so everyone in the area can claim one for a neighborhood garden plot. School classes can use these opportunities to grow plants as a learning experience. If the school has a summer program, the children can follow the growth of the seeds from the beginning to the harvest. Lessons in science, math, and even reading can revolve around the growing plants.

Become a driver for any of the field trips the classes take. Provide a history lesson. Just because you don't feel old enough to be historic, your life is much longer than that of a child.

You've seen events that they'll read about in their history books. Even if you never went to Woodstock, maybe you saved some old clothes from that era (yes, it is sad for baby-boomer parents to realize that to the schoolchildren today, Woodstock is ancient history!). Volunteer to speak about your life and experiences growing up decades before the Internet or home computers. You have an opportunity to make a difference for your schools, take the time to do it.

Government

Educating tomorrow's citizens requires more than just the dedication of teachers or the watchful eye of parents. It also requires effective government participation.

Some government intervention is just that—intervention into the learning process that helps no one and makes it more difficult for teachers to teach and children to learn.

However, there are also some actions taken by the government that help the process of learning. The state of Indiana is one of the first to protect their teachers and essentially make their classrooms more conducive for learning. Initially, troubled by the threat of frivolous suits by parents when teachers disciplined students' bad behavior, lawmakers created House Enrolled Act 1462 that offered the full services of the Indiana Attorney General's office to teachers. Then the state took a stronger stance and now gives more than just the services of the Attorney General's office, and if the discipline was reasonable and just, it makes the teacher immune from suit.

The new government regulation from the conservative area of the Midwest shows that people have had enough of the growing issue of students' rights. This doesn't mean that the student isn't important; quite the contrary. It simply means that "the people" no longer want the inmates running the asylum. It means that the government finally is helping the teacher to ensure that discipline exists in the classroom so all students can learn.

The government still doesn't see the big picture, however, when it comes to spending money. In an effort to right the wrongs of the past, they often create new wrongs, frequently to the same group of people they believed they were helping. Busing is one example of the new wrong created.

Busing was intended to give every child an equal education by mixing the races. However, what it does is simply give many of the children from lower economic neighborhoods the opportunity to see the sites of their city in their long bus ride across town. It also prevents many of these same underprivileged children from participating in after school activities and removes them from their friends and neighbors. Parents, particularly those without transportation, cannot easily travel to school functions and because of that, the child suffers and the parents receive the label of "uncaring."

Effective government should instead look at the other countries that now far excel our nation in educational accomplishments. They should look at the programs of those nations that place first emphasis on personal responsibility and then go about the process of teaching the ABCs. They should ask why our great nation lags behind countries that were once our inferiors in the area of education. Instead, we receive political promises and empty dollars thrown at the educational system in a random method.

Until America wakes up and smells the coffee, there will be no medals for the field of education. Not only are the schools catering to the few who choose to disrupt, society as a whole is also following the lead. Never before in the history of our country has stupidity and lack of responsibility been so profitable. From receiving money for spilling hot drinks into your lap to suing a store for the disruptive behavior of a child (who happens to be your own!) and winning, we have become a nation where it pays to take no personal responsibility for our life. The schools reflect this attitude and our placement in our educational effectiveness demonstrates it.

GPS 38: Final Reflections

While the analogy of a trip may seem too simple, it is fitting. Raising a family is more than a one-time effort; it is a long process and everything you do has an effect on the outcome. No matter what your race, creed or color, making sure you're behind the wheel of your family's car of life is the most important job you have.

Studies show that children with parents who are involved in their educational process do better in school. Make certain that you are one of those parents and know that you make a difference every time you participate in meetings and functions that have to do with school business.

Asking the school for help in accomplishing the trip to your child's adulthood is important. While it may be uncomfortable at first, it's no different from asking directions at a gas station when the route is unfamiliar. When it's necessary, everyone loves to help and will offer what information they can.

Controlling your emotions and acting rationally as the head of your household is just as important to parenting as it is to driving. There's an old saying that anger never makes you arrive to any destination faster, except the cemetery. If you see roadblocks in the way, respectfully question authorities and search for a way to remove them. If other drivers aren't following the rules of the road, speak up, but not in anger. No one solves anything with shouting, and calm communication promotes understanding and teamwork.

No matter what, as a parent you must always keep your eye on the destination and question whether your actions or those of others are helping you to arrive or are a diversion away from your goal. You cannot choose the final goal for another, but you do have the choice for your house, just as Joshua did. You cannot speak for others, but you have the right and the responsibility to speak for your house.

Taking charge of your own life is the key to success. Without that ability, the individual becomes a pawn to the whims of others. Without belief that the efforts of the individual count, parents are truly the leaders of the home, and that education matters, there will continue to be a downslide in our educational system.

No matter how much you work at keeping your family pointed in the right educational direction, there are always side roads to attract children, and diversions from their educational process. However, that's not always bad. In one way or another education takes place every moment of every day. The key is to be able to control the outcome of the education. In doing this you also can remain in charge of your house.

If your child finds an outside interest that you don't feel fits into the educational scheme you had planned, take a moment to examine the interest and see how you can make it work. For instance, video games seem to draw children away from studies but some of the video games provide excellent skills to use in life. Even those that entertain often stimulate the brain.

Allow only a specific amount of time each week for playing video games. When your child begs to play longer, be resolute! Many parents simply remove the game controllers and hide them somewhere safe, producing them only during approved game time. Remember: there is no law that says your child is entitled to play video games. Video game time should be a reward for good grades and good behavior.

Look for video games that offer educational skills as well as provide entertainment. Before you purchase, check the rating of the game to make certain it doesn't contain violence, nudity, or other undesirable elements.

Instead of turning your child loose on the game and allowing the game to baby-sit, participate in the game and discover how to play it yourself. By joining your child, you'll help to create bonds and in the process, keep your mind active and up to date. Dialogue is the most important part of the play as well as the camaraderie formed. You could use it as part of a new tradition of game night.

You cannot know what your child is doing every minute of the day and this often leads parents to feel out of control. But children need to grow and develop. You have to allow them to make decisions for themselves. By giving the right values through your actions and words, you've done just that. However, this doesn't mean that you simply turn them loose on the world and hope for the best.

Keep in contact with the school and participate in organizations that donate time and ideas to the operation of the school. This is one method of maintaining contact with your child but also seeing how the educational system handles many problems. Encourage other parents to do the same. When all parents unite for the common good of the children, there's a brighter educational day on the horizon.

Set limits for your child and don't budge. A child with no limits may claim to be happy, but in the back of his or her mind is the dark thought that perhaps their parents just don't care. Children need to know that you care about them. Set specific benchmarks for your child to accomplish to earn more freedom of choice. This is probably the most valuable lesson a parent can teach his or her child. With freedom comes responsibility and responsible behavior begets more freedom.

As their child develops into an adult, peer pressure is probably the most difficult hurdle for parents to overcome. The easiest way to do this is to make friends with the parents of your child's friends. If Billy wants to stay the night at Jimmy's house, meet Jimmy's parents first. Rather than have awkward moments, begin to make friends as soon as the children form the friendship. You'll know when that happens. Call the parents of the other child and invite both them and their child to a cookout. You'll have a good idea of the family unit after one evening. If you don't find the parent's rules and regulations are the same as yours, simply have Jimmy over to your house overnight instead of the reverse.

Remember—if your child chooses an inappropriate friend, try to avoid being judgmental. Just say that Jimmy or Suzie's family does things in a way that your family doesn't, and that it's the parents' job to make these tough decisions. You have nothing against Jimmy or Suzie, but you and your family must stay on track!

Knowing the parents of your child's friends is important in other ways. Kids are kids, no matter how well you raise them, and at some point Jimmy is going to say he's at your house and your child will say he's at Jimmy's house. In reality, they're both up to mischief. By knowing the parents of your child's friends, you can easily find out the fraud they intend to perpetrate on both of you. It's nothing more than a simple phone call.

Standing up for your beliefs is never a one-time shot but a continuous battle. Maintaining a consistent voice on your beliefs and values is the only way to continue to direct your house in the style of living you believe correct. If, along the way, you find that you were wrong on a previous stand, acknowledge it. Honesty, particularly to children, and the ability to change directions when proven wrong is an important value to impart. Always remember that a sign of a good parent is one who does the best they can with the information they possess at the time.

Universal moral values including self-responsibility and the right way to live don't change. They apply to every family of every economic level and social status. If you uphold your values you'll always know you gave your child the best foundation for his house—even if you have to occasionally change the color of the shutters.

What Say You?

"Upon reading *As For Me and My House* the second time, I thought it was even more brilliant than the first time I read it. What an elegant, practical, no nonsense volume. If only we could get every school board in the USA to read it."

— Erin Schmidt, *South Bend Examiner*

"In the struggle to make American education more competitive, *As For Me and My House: A GPS for Parents of School-Age Children* is a must-read for families and offers powerful solutions."

— Cynthia Carr, Parent — Hope Mills, North Carolina

"It is commonly said by teachers that parents are as much of the challenge of teaching children as any other and this book prepares parents to get the most out of their local education system."

— Book Reviews by Alan Caruba

"Having clearly identified with …the fact that education in the United States, particularly the public and pre-college varieties, is currently in a deplorable condition and getting worse, the author offers an array of solutions that range from the obvious to the provocatively controversial…. on balance, a valuable resource for parents, teachers, and students to use in their important struggle against the dark"

— Gordon Osmond, Book Pleasures.com

"The author demonstrates her deep and genuine concern for the progress of education in the country, and, …is not reluctant to address more sensitive and urgent issues as well."

— David Hughes @Amazon.com

About the Author

Rose Marie Whiteside is the creator of three websites located at http://www.inpublicschools.com, http://www.empower-education-empower.com, and http://www.mag.inpublicschools.com. A fourth has been set up dedicated to this book, http://www.as-for-me-and-my-house.com that gives an overview of the book and allows you to hear the author speak about education and the book.

A graduate of Syracuse University with dual study between political science and English literature, she also did graduate study at Syracuse in the field of special education. Her last degree came from SUNY Albany's first graduating class in social work.

Now a senior citizen, the author has worked in many fields involving children and youth in both education and juvenile justice. She has one biological son and two beautiful granddaughters. Each has been a product of both public and private schools.

www.ingramcontent.com/pod-product-compliance
Lightning Source LLC
LaVergne TN
LVHW011231080426
835509LV00005B/443